Zenvesting

"The Tao never does anything, yet through it all things are done"

TAO TE CHING

FINANCIAL
SOURCEBOOK
PUBLISHING

Suttons Bay, MI

Zenvesting

THE ART
OF
ABUNDANCE

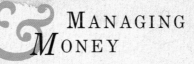

& MANAGING MONEY

PAUL H. SUTHERLAND CFP

Published by **Financial Sourcebook Publishing**
417 St. Joseph Street, PO Box 40, Suttons Bay, MI 49682

10 9 8 7 6 5 4 3 2 1

Publisher's Cataloging-in-Publication Data

Sutherland, Paul H.
    Zenvesting : the art of abundance &
managing money / Paul H. Sutherland.
  —Suttons Bay, MI : Financial Sourcebook
Pub. , Nov. 1998.

    p. cm.
Includes bibliographical references and
index.
    ISBN 0–9661060–1–6 (pbk.)
      1. Investments. 2. Finance, Personal.
3. Zen Buddhism. I. Title.

HG4521 .S88 1998
332.6—dc21

Library of Congress Catalog Card Number: 98-93141

Illustrations and design: McClellan Design, Corte Madera CA 94925

Managing Editor: Matt Sutherland

Printed on recycled paper

To order additional books, call 800.632.5528

Contents

ROMANTIC

We are born into the human family as part of an intimate oneness with nature and a conscious connection to God. Half animal, we seek food, sex, and comfort from fear; half god, we seek to feel and share harmony with all of creation.

Reality pulls us to see the fragile splendor of life, but also illuminates the sophisticated manifestations of the animal within us: to fight, run, take, hoard, dominate, hurt—just as our aboriginal kin did millions of years ago.

We also experience peace, love, kindness, happiness, ecstasy and similar ties to our Christ/Buddha nature.

Understanding that we live in these varying forms of reality, and that our environment often pulls at our basest nature, can lead to difficult conflicts. With society's help, we fall victim to unhealthy habits and unrestrained desires.

REALITY

To get into harmony with money and life we must gently resist falling under the spell of consumerism.

"All is vanity," was the cry scribed in Ecclesiastes, as if to imply that nothing is worth fretting over. Buddha preached on desireless-ness for much the same reason.

As part animal and part God, we must let reality pull us back to doing what is right simply because *it is* right; unattached to the outcome or process.

When we do what is right for ourselves and our family—without expectations—and take actions toward compassion and financial security, we will grow to manifest a harmonic synthesis of our animal and god-like nature. When pressured to believe that consumption is fulfilling—resist! Love yourself, love your family, and instead, get in harmony with your own romantic reality.

"In Zen there really aren't any doctrines. Zen isn't an ideology; it's an experience. But it isn't an experience either, because experience is always something that begs description and explanation; experience, understood as such, is ideology."

NORMAN FISCHER

My brother and editor, Matt Sutherland, called one morning midway through the compilation of this book to ask the timely question, "Paul, what is Zen?"

The fact was, the more Matt read, the more illusory Zen became.

Briefly speechless, I pondered how to answer when Matt offered, "I guess I mean, is it a religion, even? I like what I'm researching, but I can't seem to grasp the essence."

"Matt," I said, "Zen's not a religion; Zen is a way of life, of being, of thinking, or really, not being and not thinking. You can read and get refreshment from Zen even if you are a Jew, Christian, Muslim, or Atheist."

We talked a few minutes longer and Matt seemed partially relieved by the conversation. I leaned my head back and was reminded of a Churchill quote: "I don't know what I think about that until I've heard what I've had to say about that."

I was a bit shocked to realize I had never explained Zen to any-one. My years of Zen study have served me with a great deal of comfort, but very little of my understanding has ever been put to words.

I am hopeful that this book will help people and do no harm.

Aristotle said, "The young think they know everything," and while I am one-tenth as smart as I was twenty years ago, if I was sixty-three instead of forty-three, I'm sure I could not begin to write this book. My youthful ego allows me the enthusiasm to try to communicate financial principles which help people succeed financially and in life.

I hope readers will put the fundamentals and ideals within this book into practice. I realize that the wonderful Chinese philosopher Lao-Tzu was probably above the "ego need" to have his words help people, but I am not.

To my spiritual friends of various religions, please forgive me if any of my quotes seem out of context or character. My prayers will be answered if everyone is able to find good, tangible truths in *Zenvesting* that make their lives more peaceful and rewarding.

ACKNOWLEDGMENTS

To my parents, Dale and Mary, who sustained me in my youth with food, shelter, love and safety. To Kimberly, my wife and friend with love and commitment, and our children, Akasha and Keeston, who have helped me understand what is really important in life. And to Aristotle, Jesus, Buddha, Thich Nhat Hanh, Plato, Abraham Maslow, Lao-Tzu, Moses, Immanuel Kant, St. Francis, Mohatma Gandhi, Martin Luther King, Mary Baker Eddy, Susan Moon, Abraham Lincoln, Margo Anand, Benjamin Hoff, Alan Cohen, Robert Muller, Wayne Dyer, Jeff Greenwald, Susan Bondy, and Norman Fischer, and others who inspired and taught me the power of the written word. My heart and boundless respect go out to Aung San Suu Kyi who struggles today in Myanmar.

Ven. Geshe Lhundub Sopa and Geshe Kelsang Gyatsu Rinpoche whose interpretations of Lamrim instructions, Mahayana and other compassion awakening (Bodhicitta) and wisdom texts have helped me greatly. The few days I spent away from work and family to hear His Holiness The 14th Dalai Lama, Tenzin Gyatso discuss compassion Dharma, and to observe the AvalokiteshVara (Kriya tantra), empowerment and the taking of Bodhicitta and Bodhisattva vows by hundreds of Buddhist pilgrims helped make it possible to get briefly beyond my mind and into my heart, to very slightly get a glimpse of the essence of the path.

"If powerful men and women could center themselves in it, the whole world would be transformed by itself, in its natural rhythms. People would be content with their simple everyday lives, in harmony, and free of desire.

When there is no desire, all things are at peace."

TAO TE CHING

The truth is simple—money connects us; it is energy, it is beautiful, and it can do wonderful things. As a motivating force, money knows few equals; success is often measured by wealth. But how much do we need? Where is that mystical point of equilibrium which marks the boundaries of spiritual materialism? To achieve balance we must face these issues.

Be cautioned that financial enlightenment cannot be reached through dogmatic lessons or conditioned thinking patterns. Instead, perceptions must be altered slightly, a reversion is required. We are born with nothing—no opinions, belongings, good or bad habits. But soon we become fixated on useless things and foolish thoughts. Our lives ebb and flow to an invisible pull of desire. Happiness is viewed like a destination. "If only," we tell ourselves, "then I will reach my dreams." Only when we are able to clarify our thoughts back in the direction of the "buddha mind" (that state we knew as newborns) do we have an opportunity to know inner peace.

Money need not play a spoiler role in so many lives. Those compromising situations where reality plainly shows that our actions may cause suffering must be recognized and handled responsibly.

Advice given in this book is general in nature and may not specifically pertain to your needs. If you have any doubt about the information contained herein, you should seek competent financial planning advice. The onus is always on the investor to assess the risk or appropriateness of any investment strategy. It is our sincere hope that those who read this book will achieve greater financial security and live a happy and balanced life.

Paul H. Sutherland is not affiliated with any broker, dealer, bank, trust company, insurance company, insurance agency, mutual fund company, or other firm which may compensate him for referrals generated through this book. Nor are the mutual funds, discount brokers, and other companies listed in this book necessarily endorsed by the author or publisher of *Zenvesting*.

We do expect a degree of criticism from our sharp commentary of commission sales people, i.e., stock brokers selling load and commission-able mutual funds, insurance agents pushing insurance products for large commissions, and unqualified people giving financial advice. Anyone that takes offense to information in this book, should please put their criticism in writing and forward it to us so that we can review it to assure *Zenvesting* is accurate and truthful.

Our address: P.O. Box 40, 417 St. Joseph Street, Suttons Bay, MI 49682
Our E-mail: pub@fimg.net
Our Phone Number: 800 632-5528 or 616 271-3915

1

MY VERY BEING

I take up space, I breathe. My very being affects the ecosystem in innumerable, sometimes harmful ways but I am here; no better than Hitler, no worse than Jesus or Buddha. I do what I think is right at my own level of consciousness, humbly realizing my limitations and humanness. My essence and actions can bring peace, harmony, love, joy, beauty, prosperity, tolerance, and spiritual responsibility in each direction I travel.

Read the above prayer again. Feel it. The spirit of the prayer is a vital connection to the message in this book—as if it were the kindness that fortifies a smile.

Zen teachings do not necessarily conflict with the practice of religion. They have peacefully co-existed for millions of people and thousands of years. Only where beliefs and obsessive rituals pre-dispose a believer against elemental truths are there grounds for anyone to take issue with the Zen way. Zen is most concerned with a living reality. Growing, moving, observing. Never an exclusionary policy, as is prevalent in other religions.

Don't be saddened by your human limitations. Know you are here and feel grateful for each breath of life. Close your eyes. Take a breath and feel the air move through your nose, down into your lung linings. Acknowledge the pleasure. Air. Wonderful, underappreciated air. If we were forced to pay for our daily breaths we would certainly place more value on this most passionate element of life, so taken for granted.

You may be wondering what this has to do with money. Play along. We need to find our center and feel completely serene, wholly peaceful with our breathing. (Be careful, the sudden infusion of a lover's scent may cause your knees to buckle.) The key elements of balance and finding your center that underscore this chapter are vital to your understanding of money. Like food, water, warmth, and touch, money is part of our lives. View it like energy.

But in order to handle the

"For innumerable eons, I have preferred the superficial to the fundamental, drifting through various states of existence, creating much animosity and hatred, bringing endless harm and discord. Though I have done nothing wrong in this life, I am reaping the natural consequences of past offenses, my evil karma. It is not meted out by some heavenly agency. I accept it patiently and with contentment, utterly without animosity or complaint."

BODHIDHARMA

energy generated by money, it is necessary to have a balanced view of life. Concentrating on every breath helps us maintain awareness of our existence. This awareness also keeps us humble and fulfilled, so we can enjoy the feeling of holding a crying baby as it gasps for air and learns to interact with a new world.

Are you starting to understand? All aspects of life are wonderful. Feel. Think. Emote. Sleep. Wake. Cry. Gain. Lose.Enjoy it all, savor it, experience it.

Of course our very being uses resources, but we can lessen our impact on the world by respecting life, practicing tolerance, recycling, and loving unconditionally, unequivocally.

Do you know what you want?
Do you know what you have?

Most of us haven't a clue about what we want, but generally think of pleasure and suffering as emotions to seek out or avoid. The ready pursuit of pleasure presents us with one of the top laws in nature: actions have consequences. Jesus said, "Whatsoever a man soweth, that shall he reap." In fact, we are surrounded by reminders of the benefits of kindness and upstanding behavior. At some point in our maturity, we forgo the need to attach a carrot to our acts of benevolence. We realize that kindness and honesty are their own rewards, regardless of our personal gain. We must also acknowledge the strain caused by our unseemly behavior: our behavior should be consistent with what is right and in harmony with our needs.

Understanding who you are is based on your commitments. Your everyday actions speak louder than any good intentions you may have. Your actions reflect a decision you have made. Hold tight to that decision. Does it reflect you?

Creating A Gentle Budget

Years ago, I remember asking my father why he didn't aspire to be superintendent of schools, a job with a much higher pay than his principal's salary. He had been offered the position, he acknowledged, but turned it down because

he was reluctant to spend more time being involved in the politics of the job. He admitted to being a hopeless family man and hugged me, scratching his scruffy face against mine.

As you might imagine, my parent's "good money" budget included used cars and a home completed by the labor of six kids managing paint brushes, hammers, and skilsaws. There was no extra money to fund a college account or family vacations, and hand-me-down clothing was the norm.

A tradeoff my parents made was to move from a large city in southern Michigan to a resort area, so we would have access to lakes, forests, and outdoor activities, as well as summer jobs at seasonal restaurants. I could not imagine a better environment to be raised in.

When making decisions about commitments, certain financial matters come into play. The following chapter will be more specific about budgets, but the first step in a Gentle Budget is to take into account your commitments. Write them down. (For example, I am committed to: doing no harm, financial security for my family, honesty, love, truth, having a balanced life, and so on.)

I am committed to:

_____
_____
_____
_____
_____
_____
_____
_____
_____
_____
_____
_____
_____
_____
_____
_____
_____
_____

"Whatsoever things are true, whatsoever things are honest, whatsoever things are just, whatsoever things are pure, whatsoever things are lovely - think on these things."

PHILIPPIANS 4:8

Now let's quantify your list by assigning it some meaning, because how you spend your time is a very good indication of your priorities. For example, if you prioritize a wonderful marriage, you are committed to spending ample time with your spouse, remaining faithful, and learning about relationships.

Donating time to those less fortunate may be another priority. List a few of them:

Priority: _____
Commitment : _____

Priority: _____
Commitment : _____

Priority: _____
Commitment : _____

Priority: _____
Commitment : _____

Priority: _____
Commitment : _____

With your list of priorities in mind and the commitments necessary to achieve them, you can easily schedule an ideal day of activities. This task will not only contribute to your sense of "centering," but also address a level of discipline and an accompanying sense of accomplishment. How will you spend your time living up to your spiritual obligations? Will you turn from your priorities? These are the real telling choices of your life.

Of Budgets and Bliss: Achieving Cooperation

Young relationships often catch the brunt of financial anxiety; incomes are lower, savings non-existent, and household expenditures are ever present. Indeed, incorporating restraint and diplomacy into the cauldron of new love can be a difficult task.

The *way* to tranquility in relationships, much like achieving balance in other aspects of your life, is the essence of Zen, often mistaken for passivity. In his extensive writings, Lao-Tzu emphasizes softness or adaptability; not inactivity. By letting go of expectations, judgments, and desires, we become in harmony with the way things are.

In terms of budgets, the starting point is to fill out the budget sheet **Figure 1.1,** showing your income and expenses. After a few months of monitoring your expenses, you will have a better understanding of the flow of money.

In terms of relationships, one intriguing theory, Imago Therapy, is based on the work of Dr. Harville Hendrix. Imago focuses on a persons natural desire for self completion, especially as it relates to unsettled childhood issues. In adulthood, we are inexorably attracted to partners who confront us with the same dilemmas we faced as children desperate for an opportunity to work things out. Of course we end up attached to someone very much the same as our parents; an ideal person to not meet our needs.

Before I was privy to the theories of Dr. Hendrix, I could take constructive criticism by others, but was very sensitive to any criticism from my loving wife. That criticism would send me into the emotional state of a four-year-old—I could not see it objectively.

"You're going to mail that to your editor," she might say, and I would begin to boil. With anger and expletives, I'd reply "Of course I was going to mail it, but now I'll just throw it in the trash."

At which time she would be allowed to finish her thought, "It's a great article but I'm sure you're going to need another stamp."

Imago (literally, an "image" of the person who can complete you) Therapy helped me realize that it was something stimulated from my parents that made me react in a defensive manner. I can now talk to Kim without worrying about loss of love or rejection.

I want to – must have – a balanced life. I live for harmony and bliss. I can tell my partner anything because I know they trust, love, and are committed to me. I realize that we have time! I realize that we have money! I realize that we trade time for money, but I need guidance to achieve a balance in my life, a blissful point where my needs and my family's needs are met realistically, consciously, and comfortably. Help me to learn to cooperate, balance, compromise, to live my life

"Karma - all that total of a soul which is the things it did, the thoughts it had, the 'self it wove."

SIR
EDWIN
ARNOLD

1.1 Trading Time for Money: Monthly Budget Sheet

	Month 1	Month 2	Month 3	Month Average
INCOME Total/Month				
EXPENSES				
House/Rent payments				
Home Insurance				
Property Taxes				
Car Payments				
Auto Expenses				
Phone (personal)				
Electricity/Heating				
Food				
Child Care				
Entertainment				
Holiday				
Sanity: *(yoga, counseling)*				
Fun:*(wine, cigars, latte)*				
Personal Development				
Helping Others				
Tithing				
Insurance *(life, health, home)*				
2nd Home				
Net Investment Expenses				
Home Maintenance				
Credit Cards				
Other				
TOTAL EXPENSES				
(Subtract EXPENSE from INCOME total)				
A **Total/Month for investment & income tax**				
B **Income Tax**				
SURPLUS/DEFICIT Subtract **B** from **A**				

*consistent with my responsibilities
and commitments.*

Snap out of it. Stop feeling
sorry for yourself. Relationships
are no picnic, but you can't wait
around expecting something for
nothing. And furthermore, you are
not your parents, your partner is
not your parent, and opposites
attract: It is logical that you will
fall in love with someone who
brings out your full range of
emotions, both good and uncomfortable. Let these emotional
responses flow through you, see
where they come from, know their
source, and laugh about it. Emotions are reality and they are wonderful!

*Now breathe. Again, please. Close
your eyes and think about the
meaning your relationship brings
into your life. About all the pleasure
in simple things, like holding a
hand. Breathe.*

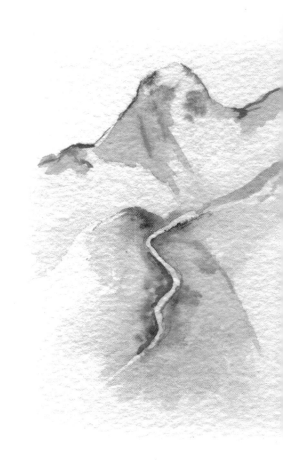

2 WAKE UP & SMELL
THE KARMA

It's karma, not debt. That credit card balance: karma. This notion may require a radical shift in viewpoint, but you must take responsibility for your actions, especially when the alternatives are as painful as bad credit reports or bankruptcy. Go ahead and coddle yourself momentarily, blame societal pressure and easy credit for your financial difficulties, then get on with a solution. There is no quick fix.

The goal is to manage your debt consistently with the reality of your life. Here are three straightforward steps to help you get out of debt (karma) trouble:

1. Realize your debt is your problem, caused by your actions.
2. Forgive yourself and move forward. Own up to the idea that you are responsible, that karma exists. Hopefully that will slow you down before you spend next month's rent.
3. Take your debt very seriously. Make it a very real part of your life. Loans, credit cards, etcetera, are wonderful tools which help us enjoy life, though too much is like too much ice cream; it makes you sick.

Debt Dharma

Dharma:"The Ultimate law of all things"

Ideally, balanced and healthy spending habits are acquired at an early age, so that you can avoid a cumbersome debt load or *debtors prison* (that state of mind which makes it hard to smile and breath comfortably). While old habits are hard to break, the following ten rules will keep you from mismanaging income, assets, and debt. If you play it straight you can be virtually assured of a more balanced life.

RULE ONE

Put away enough liquid assets to equal six months budget, before you go into debt. This means that if your total monthly expenses (including mortgage, school loans, charity, savings, food, entertainment, utilities, EVERYTHING) total $4000, you need to accumulate $24,000 as a security valve.

"The Buddha said that it is possible for us to be peaceful and happy in the present moment. That is the teaching of trista dharma sadha vihara. It means living happiliy in the present moment."

THICH NHAT
HANH

Therefore, if you earn $5000 monthly ($1000 surplus each month) and want a new car that costs $400 a month, you should have the down payment in savings so as not to dip into your security fund. Feel free to consider CDs and conservative mutual funds as liquid assets when faced with setting up your reserve fund, and it's okay to borrow. Stock portfolios, on the other hand, should be counted on for half their current value.

RULE TWO
Work to increase your monthly "divine surplus." Depending on the security of your job, a surplus of between 10% and 40% is good. Self-employed individuals would be wise to save upwards of 25% if possible, due to the sometimes unstable nature of the work, while those employed by the government, for instance, can usually get away with a 10% surplus.

RULE THREE
Total debt payments should not exceed one-third of your income. No more than 25% should go to housing (mortgage or rent), while 10% or so for auto and other debt installment payments is appropriate.

RULE FOUR
Think balance – life is forever. Debt is not a portender of the road to ruin. Don't be convinced that a debt free life is an ideal. Karma does not work that way. Consolidate your home, investment properties, home improvements, and other long term assets into one big loan with a fixed rate and the minimum required payment. (Quickly go on to Rule 5.)

RULE FIVE
Take full advantage of the fact that home loan interest is deductible. To understand the benefit of restructuring your debt to take advantage of this, see **Figure 2.1.**

RULE SIX
Never pay down your home interest rate by paying points. Instead, go for a fixed rate, fifteen to thirty year mortgage that has no points. The idea is to always allow yourself to refinance when interest rates fall.

RULE SEVEN
Aspire to be your own banker by

2.1 Debt Restructure

Asset	Value	Loan	Payment
Home (existing)	$250,000	$110,000	$1,250.00
Auto No. 1 (existing)	$15,000	$14,000	$323.00
School Loan (existing)	Priceless	$10,000	$245.00
6 Month Budget	See First Rule	$36,000	To Liquid Savings
To replace car in 3 years:*	(new need)	$20,000 in liquid savings	
Total needed to consolidate debts	Build liquidity	$190,000	

Enlightened Debt Management

Asset	Value	Loan	Payment
Home	$250,000	$190,000	30 yr. fixed @ 9%=$1,250

* Note: Save $300 monthly to liquid account to anticipate buying new car in future.

paying cash for cars, boats, etcetera. When anticipating a large purchase, begin saving to a liquid account so that when the time comes, ample cash is available.

RULE EIGHT

Maintain control over your "instant karma" cards (credit cards). Again, like other debt vehicles, credit cards offer wonderful freedom. And quite often there are frequent flyer miles to accrue, charities to benefit, and other perks accompanying credit card usage without modifying behavior. Be careful, debtors prison is very quickly accessed through credit cards. Adhere to the following dharma for help in balanced credit card usage: 1) If you can't use them responsibly, cut them up and cancel them. 2) Pay off the balance each month.

RULE NINE

Keep promises, even at difficult moments when the pressure to consume is strongest. Don't play the irresponsible game of justifying aberrant spending behavior as someone else's fault. If you sign the loan application, accept the credit card, or close the deal with the car dealer, it's your karma to live up the commitment, each and every payment. Occasionally, legitimate problems arise and it is necessary to appeal to your banker for relief. They are prepared for calls like this, so don't wait too long.

RULE TEN

Don't wait till you lose your job or have a medical crisis to get your debt/liquidity life in order; do it now! Banks will loan you money when you "don't need it" so to speak, but too often decline when difficulties arise. This is reality.

"*a*BUNDANCE IN ALL THINGS—material, emotional, intellectual, spiritual—is the goal of any first-rate soul. But into which of those categories does money fit? Automatically, you say 'material.' Uncle Larry disagrees. Uncle Larry says *'spiritual.'* Money may be our greatest spiritual teacher. More edifying than a stadium full of swamis.

Nothing can knock a pilgrim off the path as fast as money.

That's the job of a spiritual teacher, you know.

Not to hold us on the path, but to knock us off of it. Until we can stay on the path without ever being knocked—or tempted—off, until we can resist the teacher's carrot and withstand his rod, our transformative journey can be little more than fits and starts. When it comes to illuminating the inner structure of consciousness and highlighting its weaknesses and flaws, nothing,

not even love, casts as bright a beam as money. The things we're willing to do to obtain it, to protect it, to express our guilt over having it, are incomparably revealing. There's a thin line between charity and greed: at bottom, they're both expressions of insecurity and manifestations of ego. If you want to know how insecure you are, how swollen and stiff your ego is, what your chances are of staying on the path, just examine your attitudes toward the juice. Money's a terrible servant but a wonderful master. Far be it from Uncle Larry, my dear, to come between a seeker and her guru."

TOM ROBBINS

SOWING SEEDS:
ENLIGHTENED INVESTING
FOR THE FUTURE

3

Do Good with Your Money?

Scholars of old talk about the notion of no time – no past, no future, only now; this exact moment is all we have. All of the past, future, and now is present in this moment, and we cycle through this reality of "no time" with clocks (of all things) to help us distinguish past/present/future.

Life itself is a cycle; the rising and setting sun, blooming and withering flowers, the various highs and lows of human beings, ebbing and flowing tides, all as natural as can be.

In their rising and falling, ebbing and flowing nature, financial markets are equally as cyclical. Economists can point to influences like human psychology, interest rates, business cycles, currency variations, et cetera, to describe why financial markets jump around, but they are unable to pinpoint why these markets are cyclical. They simply go up and down because money and markets are a vital part of life.

Investors who wish to build their wealth can use the ebb and flow of financial cycles. For example, the stock market over time has tended to rise powerfully, only to settle back down into a neutral state of balance followed by a downturn then a general reversal of the process. In fact, there are great tools to measure the stock market cycles: follow the dividend yields.

The variations in yields that the stock market has paid have been a solid portender of when to be in the market and when to stay on the sidelines.

Simple Cycles of Dividends

The stock market is cheap when dividend yields are over 5% and conversely, it's time to sell when yields get down under 3% or so. This may be the most logically oriented way to gauge the financial markets and manage your portfolio.

In order to stay current and appropriately invested for tomorrow, you must open your mind and always try to purchase assets that appear undervalued. A sound strategy must balance the financial risks of investing with the opportunity that is created by market volatility and its cyclical nature.

Successfully managing investments can be as hard as managing a romance. Luckily you can delegate a large part of your investment management to a professional, should you feel the need. Otherwise, a well constructed portfolio of top quality mutual funds is the answer.

Whichever way you choose, you are responsible for your investment success. Do not place your financial security in the hands of a manager, mutual funds, an intuitive friend, or anyone but yourself. Delegating this responsibility to a good fee-only manager

with experience is fine, but you are then responsible to check out and monitor your manager. Acknowledge this very important responsibility before you delve further into this chapter.

If your portfolio is under $250,000, and especially if you are a "control your karma" devotee, a portfolio of mutual funds managed under the following market cycle system is best. For larger portfolios, consult the section on Financial Experts to guide you to a good professional wealth manager.

Investments can be categorized into two polarities: short-term, less volatile investments and long-term, more volatile investments. A short-term investment need might be a six-month safety reserve of income for emergencies, or money to buy a car or to go on vacation. Money for this purpose is best invested in a quality no-load money market fund with low cost or free checking; choose either a taxable or tax-free fund, depending upon your individual tax situation. A long-term investment need, on the other hand, is constructing a carefully conceived long term

3.1 S & P 500 Dividend Yield & Future Stock Market Performance

S&P 500 Yield	6 Months	1 Year	2 Years	3 Years
Below 3%	-1%	-5%	-10%	-1%
3 to 4%	+1%	+4%	+9%	+12%
4 to 5%	+7%	+14%	+21%	+26%
5 to 6%	+4%	+11%	+33%	+56%
6 to 7%	+6%	+12%	+32%	+45%
Above 7%	+8%	+29%	+42%	+63%

retirement portfolio to assure income in the future.

Families should have safety reserves of four to twelve months' budget invested in safe, easily accessible, no-load money market investments, or no-load short-term bond funds, with easy access through check writing privileges. The relative safety and security make short-term investments popular, although these predictable qualities (and low interest rates) can commit the portfolio to failure due to the eroding effects of inflation and taxes.

Similarly, with a T-bill or insured CD, you know what your interest will be and you always know that you'll get your principal back. But realize that after inflation and taxes, these investments are often losers.

Investment portfolios, to be successful, must be constructed to fulfill your needs, and allow you to sleep at night. While it's easy in theory to construct a long-term portfolio designed to offset inflation, the inherent volatility of this type of portfolio can cause undue stress to some investors. In evaluating

3.2 Dividends in History		
Date	S&P 500 Dividend Yield	S&P 500 Change
August 31, 1929	2.87%	-59.2% over 21 months
May 31, 1946	3.55%	-30.1% over 19 months
March 31, 1961	2.98%	-20.0% over 15 months
January 5, 1973	2.96%	-43.0% over 22 months
August 25, 1987	2.78%	-33.0% over 3½ months
July 16, 1990	3.28%	-19.0% over 3 months

Dividend yields throughout history have been a good indicator of future stock market performance.

investments, first look at risk; how much can you stand? Risk can be minimized by using various tools of investing such as asset allocation, diversification, security analysis, and active management.

Volatile investments have positive characteristics (dividends, appreciation, long-term performance) and negative ones (volatility, business risk). Your portfolio must utilize a diversified selection of carefully chosen bargain investments.

STOCKS

Let's look objectively at stock and the stock market. Stocks can

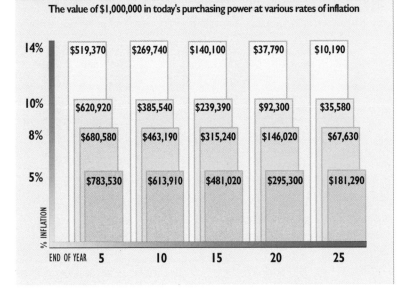

3.3 Investment vs. Inflation

The value of $1,000,000 in today's purchasing power at various rates of inflation

% INFLATION	END OF YEAR 5	10	15	20	25
14%	$519,370	$269,740	$140,100	$37,790	$10,190
10%	$620,920	$385,540	$239,390	$92,300	$35,580
8%	$680,580	$463,190	$315,240	$146,020	$67,630
5%	$783,530	$613,910	$481,020	$295,300	$181,290

represent ownership of a portfolio of US government bonds, a company trying to turn lead into gold, or stocks owning stocks. Mutual funds are a type of stock that can own stocks.

The most common perception of investing in stocks is to own interest in a corporation that will grow, increase their dividends, and prosper throughout the years. You can choose to invest in companies that are big and well established like IBM, or small companies that you hope will become big in the future; Microsoft and McDonalds are prime examples. Again, like other investments, the most important criteria in evaluating stocks is risk; it cannot be avoided when you choose to invest. But as a reward for bearing risk, an investor – with a well-constructed portfolio – should realize a favorable return.

In managing the risk of investments, the primary goal should be to avoid the purchase of assets whose prices are significantly overvalued due to manias. John Maynard Keynes became very wealthy by understanding how important psychology is in determining investment values. When describing money managers in his book *The General Theory of Employment Interest Rates and Money* (New York, Harcourt Brace Jovanovich, 1936), he said, "They are concerned not with what the investment is really worth to a man who buys it (for keeps) but with what the market will value it under the influence of mass psychology."

People invest in stocks for positive returns from dividends and capital appreciation. Some stocks don't pay out any of their earnings in dividends, but reinvest all their earnings back into the company for continued growth. These companies assume they will eventually pay dividends when the company matures. People are willing to invest in them, assuming that at some future date they will be well rewarded with significant dividends and capital appreciation. History has consistently shown this to be true.

A self-managed portfolio of mutual funds should earn enough to keep pace with inflation while minimizing risk and optimizing your chances of attaining your goals. **Figure 3.6** details investor types and dividend yields to give an overall picture of how to proceed as a Do-It-Yourself investor.

In structuring a portfolio (or in hiring a money manager) you need to address your risk tolerance first. Investment strategies should be flexible and designed to capitalize on each cycle. If the market plunges from 8,000 on the Dow to 4,000, it does not mean that you

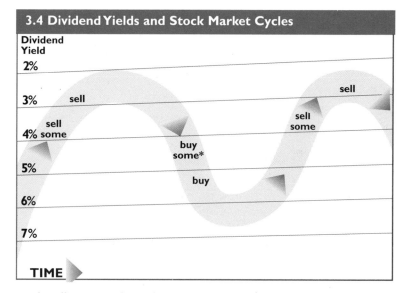

3.4 Dividend Yields and Stock Market Cycles

Dividend Yield

2%
3% sell
4% some sell some
5%
6%
7%

sell
sell some
buy some*
buy

TIME

can handle more risk just because the stock market is selling at half price; nothing guarantees that it won't go down another 50%. Probability and statistics surely suggest that there is less risk, yet a person's risk tolerance remains unchanged. You must trust your strategy and not sell out at the bottoms and buy at the tops.

Markets have – at extremes – reached dividend yields of over 7% and under 2%. Thus, under the Do-It-Yourself market cycle strategy, you might buy at a yield of 5%

Note: Over time the stock market has trended up at approximately 7% with approximately 5% of its 12% return from dividends. People who were wise enough to buy stocks when yields were at or over 5% had three year returns of over 50% on average between 1928 and the mid 1990s. Those investors who decided to hold onto stocks and try to ride out the cycles, even when yields were below 3%, earned -1% for the following three years. As with all things, "There is a time to sow and a time to reap."

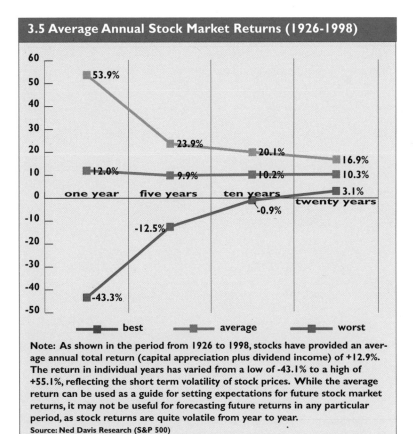

3.5 Average Annual Stock Market Returns (1926-1998)

best   **average**   **worst**

Note: As shown in the period from 1926 to 1998, stocks have provided an average annual total return (capital appreciation plus dividend income) of +12.9%. The return in individual years has varied from a low of -43.1% to a high of +55.1%, reflecting the short term volatility of stock prices. While the average return can be used as a guide for setting expectations for future stock market returns, it may not be useful for forecasting future returns in any particular period, as stock returns are quite volatile from year to year.

Source: Ned Davis Research (S&P 500)

and stick to your strategy.

The crucial decision each investor must make is how much pain or volatility is tolerable. If you trusted the management technique and your $1,000,000 portfolio lost 10% of its value, is that tolerable? What about 20%? Everyone has a threshold, even money managers. The greater the volatility that you are willing to accept, the greater the time commitment to that portfolio strategy and the greater your need for patience.

The Do-It-Yourself market cycle strategy is structured to reward you if you can tolerate some risk and volatility to your portfolio. For example, a portfolio that can handle 25% volatility should do significantly better over time than a portfolio that can only handle 5% volatility. The goal in investing is to enhance your purchasing power (versus inflation) consistent with your tolerance for risk. You must decide how much variability of return you can handle.

This is a difficult and elusive concept, one that requires investor maturity. Quite often we don't know how much volatility we can

and see your portfolio decreasing in value to reach a 7% dividend yield. Conversely, if you sell at a 3% yield it doesn't mean the markets won't go to 2% yields. Be patient

handle. If you believe you can tolerate only 5% volatility (a potential 5% loss) over a 3-5 year period, then you would be considered a risk adverse or volatility adverse investor. If you can tolerate 35-40% volatility to your portfolio, your risk tolerance is very high (you can handle a tremendous amount of variability of return). With this high risk tolerance you could expect a lot better performance over time – as long as you are patient and committed to a strategy that rewards patience. Keep in mind that the greater the volatility you are willing to accept, the greater the need for patience and time commitment.

The main problem with stocks is that they fluctuate in value. They would be a wonderful investment if their value only increased. Despite their volatility, over time, stocks have been one of the best investment classes. There has never been a 25-year period where stocks have given a return of less than 3%. The average over most 25 year periods has been a 10% return per year (which is about 7% more than inflation over the same time period). Stocks, however, do become significantly overvalued at times. This was true in 1929 and the period preceding the significant bear market of '73–'74 and '87.

Figure 3.5 illustrates how patience can be very rewarding. For example, the stock market's best 20-year period is a positive 16.7% compounded return. The worst 20-year period is a positive 3% return. The poorest 10-year period lost 1%

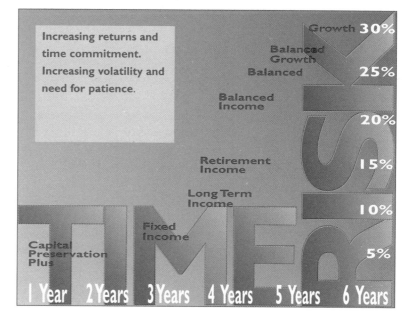

Abstain from speech and obey the spontaneity of your nature. A violent wind does not last for a whole morning; a sudden rain does not last for the whole day. To whom is it that these things are owing? To Heaven and Earth. If Heaven and Earth cannot make such spasmodic actings last long, how much less can you!

TAO TE CHING

a year, while the best 10-year period showed a 20% increase yearly. The best and worst 5-year period lost 11.9% per year and increased 23.9% a year, while the 1-year numbers are -43.1% and +55.1%. Stocks, which are the most volatile asset class, favor investors with patience.

Your money, however, needs to be wisely managed to assure that it always works as hard as possible for you. Take the initiative to develop an investment strategy that offers you a good chance of success over time. There are no guarantees. Risk can only be measured by the past, yet it only exists in the future. The notion that you can develop a strategy based specifically on historical correlation and historical data is as foolish as those who believed that man would never fly. The best investments for Do-It-Yourself investors – to minimize risk and maximize returns – is to use a portfolio of diversified mutual funds, trusts, and stocks (choose companies that are well-diversified in business makeup and socially responsible if you are so inclined). These finan-

cial investment tools are best suited for individuals reluctant to use a portfolio manager, and are effective for portfolio amounts between $1,000 and $500,000. Hiring a fee-only socially conscious professional money manager when investing amounts over $250,000 can be more cost effective than mutual funds, but make sure you hire a professional who prices their services competitively. The goal of active management is to reduce the volatility on the downside. The Do-It-Yourself strategy emphasizes risk reduction. As assets become significantly overvalued, you sell. To increase wealth coming out of a period where the stock market has performed very poorly, you buy. As mentioned earlier, stocks historically have not done well following periods where the dividend yield on the Dow Jones or the S&P 500 has averaged under 3%. On the other hand, stocks have performed incredibly well when their yields have been over 5%. The Do-It-Yourself strategy uses only the dividend yield as a bellwether to re-balancing your portfolio. To

1. Look up your investor-type (based on willingness to take risk).

2. Consult a financial newspaper or visit www.zenvesting.com to look up the dividend yield – the pie chart gives the recommended percentages to diversify your portfolio.

3. A list of socially responsible mutual funds and discount brokers is found at the end of this chapter. Worksheets to help monitor your portfolio are contained in the Investor Resources section at the back of the book.

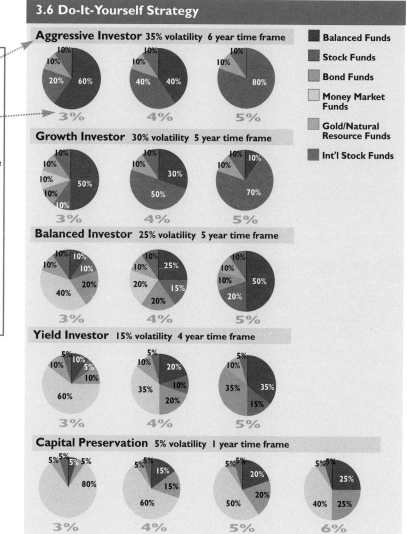

3.6 Do-It-Yourself Strategy

Aggressive Investor 35% volatility 6 year time frame

Growth Investor 30% volatility 5 year time frame

Balanced Investor 25% volatility 5 year time frame

Yield Investor 15% volatility 4 year time frame

Capital Preservation 5% volatility 1 year time frame

Balanced Funds
Stock Funds
Bond Funds
Money Market Funds
Gold/Natural Resource Funds
Int'l Stock Funds

reiterate, the Do-It-Yourself strategy which is broadly defined in **Figure** 3.6, expects you to follow five rules:

1. Use mutual funds or diversified trust funds.
2. Conclusively decide what portfolio strategy you wish to commit to for the stated period.
3. Review periodically what the yield is on the Dow Jones Industrial average or the S&P 500 average.
4. Never put more than 5% of your assets into any one investment, unless you choose a very well diversified mutual fund.
5. Review your portfolio quarterly.

The Do-It-Yourself portfolio also requires that you will completely modify your portfolio if dividend yields fall or rise. Also stay particularly responsive while dividend yields are moving one way or the other (either coming up from 3% or down from 5%).

Dividend yields tend to change very slowly over time. If the stock market suddenly drops 30% in one day, however, you should check your yields. Similarly, if the stock market seems to march ahead (upwards) day after day – and the last time you checked the yields it was at 3.5% – it is probably a good idea to find out whether the dividend yield has crossed the 3% yield threshold again. Using history as a guide, this portfolio strategy should not require you to rebalance your portfolio more than once or twice a year.

It is very important that once

3.7 About as Bad as It Gets

Objective	Loss at the '74 bottom	# of funds
Asset Allocation	-23.9%	3
Balanced	-25.8%	2
Financial	-49.9%	2
Growth	-45.2%	21
Growth & Income	-35.6%	11
Equity Income	-32.6%	3
Small Co.	-41.4%	2
Bond	-21.6%	6
World Equity	-22.0%	1
Average Loss	-33.1%	51

Note: While there were 306 mutual funds around during this period, only 51 supplied information to Morningstar for this study.

Data: Morningstar Advanced Analytics/John Smith's Financially Speaking

you decide on a strategy, you stick to it for at least five years. Stay committed, even when you are pressured by friends and business acquaintances. If you want to speculate or have some "pet" investments, it's best to set aside 80%-90% of your nest egg in a Do-It-Yourself portfolio and then play with the other 10%-20%. It is, however, very appropriate to have your portfolio critiqued by other professional money managers. If you own a lot of mutual funds, have your individual funds reviewed by someone familiar with them, and get their recommendations in writing.

When you carry out a portfolio review, I recommend hiring a fee-only money manager who will take the time to make sure that your portfolio is consistent with your goals and adheres to an appropriate strategy. You may also be served by asking them to read this book.

You should also review the investments in your portfolio on a quarterly basis to see whether they have performed "in the ballpark" of similar mutual fund types. For example, if you have three balanced mutual funds in your portfolio and one paid you an average of 10% for the last 12 months, one 15%, and the last 2%, you should first address the poorest performing fund to find out why it is not delivering up to expectations. Don't hesitate to call the mutual fund or review their annual or quarterly report to find the answer. Consider replacing the fund if their ideologies have changed. If you find the fund has been investing inappropriately, put it on the "death watch." When you need to re-balance your portfolio, replace that fund first. And, of course, diversify.

During your quarterly mutual fund review, check to make sure the same company (and individual) is still managing your portfolio. Also, check to see that their fees and investment goals have not changed during the last few months. If anything is different, you may want to consider selling that particular fund and moving your money to another fund of the same type.

Most mutual funds are extremely diversified and generally

Failure is an opportunity.
If you blame someone else,
there is no end to the blame.

Therefore the Master
fulfills her own obligations
and corrects her own mistakes.
She does what she needs to do
and demands nothing of others.

TAO TE CHING,

Evaluation Letter to Account Broker

Dear (name of broker):

I am considering setting up an account with your company, and will use predominantly open- and closed-end mutual funds to construct my portfolio. Will you allow me to buy no-load mutual funds? (Send me a list of those funds.)

What load mutual funds will you hold in my account on my behalf, if I already own some ?

Can I buy individually listed stocks? Bonds? CDs, et cetera? What money market fund do you automatically invest my cash balance in?

Do you have no-transaction-fee funds (NTF)? If so, send me details. Please send me a letter addressing the above questions. In addition, I would also like to have verification that you are a member of the Securities Investors Protection Corporation and members of a Stock Exchange and thus regulated by their rules and regulations. Please send me your corporation's latest annual report and latest quarterly report. I'd like to receive every quarterly and annual report from your company, so that I can monitor your company's financial strength.

In your letter, please outline your confidentiality safeguards, and state that you will not sell my name to anyone for solicitation of investment products or other services.

In your new investor packet, please include the following:
1. A commission schedule so that I can get an accurate idea of what it will cost to transact business through your company.
2. The name of a contact person that I may call to get more information.
3. A sample copy of your monthly portfolio statements. Will you list all my mutual funds on my monthly statement, in addition to my other assets?

I'm interested in having a relationship with you only if you will hold all my investment assets in one street name or master account.

In addition, will your company allow me check writing privileges on my non-retirement portfolio? Can you issue a VISA debit card, or other debit card? What are the costs of each of these?

Thank you for your earliest attention to the above.
Sincerely,
(Prospective Account Holder)

follow the 5% rule – no more than 5% of assets are placed in one security or investment. Knowing this, I am still biased toward having no more than 10% of my money in any one growth fund, period.

I am partial to working with a discount brokerage firm specializing in diversified portfolios (stocks, bonds, mutual funds, CDs, treasury bills, et cetera), or a bank or trust company which will allow you to have a diversified portfolio at a minimum cost. In my practice we use a SIPC-insured discount brokerage company that allows us flexibility and charges low commissions. Low commission rates (when purchasing securities) and no-load mutual funds minimize the cost associated with investing and maximize your returns. If you can reduce your fee costs by even 1%, for example, using no-load mutual funds, avoiding high brokerage commissions or high trust company fees, it translates into money that will help offset inflation and increase your financial security.

Included at the end of this chapter is a short list of very good

discount brokers that are:

1. SIPC-insured.
2. Regulated by the New York Stock Exchange and other major exchanges.
3. Carry insurance in excess of $500,000 per portfolio.

This is the short list of my criteria for safe brokers. To choose a broker who is appropriate, I suggest you send the letter on page 28.

If your portfolio is a pension or IRA rollover, you need to find out whether the broker will send you monthly checks; and if that service is free. If it's a personal account and registered in your own name or a trust, you'll also want to know how they allow you to access that account;

1. By writing checks
2. Through a VISA debit card
3. Monthly checks mailed to you.

Find out the cost of these services.

My bias toward discount brokers stems from the fact that many commission-oriented brokers tend to solicit you for business and can often get you off track, or away from your safety-first portfolio. Usually they do this at your weakest point. It may be when your portfolio has under-performed for a few quarters, and you're plainly frustrated. Discount brokers, on the other hand, simply execute your orders. Due to the increasingly competitive nature of the industry, most of them continue to offer new products and surprisingly good service at a fraction of what the full service brokers cost.

Busy investors need a simple, efficient, convenient place to safe-keep their assets. Many brokerage firms, and a few bank trust departments, have responded to this need by establishing central asset management accounts, often called cash management accounts (CMAs), or financial management accounts.

Some accounts will allow you to margin your securities if you need quick cash and don't want to sell your investments. They will also send you a tax summary at year-end listing all of your tax information, to facilitate filing your tax return. As mentioned earlier, some of the major brokerage firms have CMAs, though I find them inconvenient and

expensive for the Do-It-Yourself investor, or the investor who uses a professional money manager. Merrill Lynch, Sun America, Shearson Lehman, Dean Witter, and the like often charge high fees and commissions for such services, while restricting your use of mutual funds. In addition, these brokerage firms often have sales people pitching a new investment product, which can distract you from your investment goals.

Remember brokerage firms make money by developing and selling new products; you must decide your own strategy and stick to it. These sales calls can disrupt your long term financial security.

Mutual Funds

The trillion-dollar mutual fund industry has done wonders for individual investors. Mutual funds add a tremendous amount of efficiency and leverage, while reducing risk and offering professional management. Their popularity, however, has created a difficult problem. The over 7,000 funds that now exist are each designed to fulfill many different goals. Unsuspecting, inexperienced consumers find them contradictory and confusing. Typical mutual fund literature lists three primary advantages:

1. Diversification.
2. Professional management.
3. Lower expenses.

The mutual funds discussed and listed in this book were generally chosen to help you achieve your goals by reducing risk through proper diversification and to follow "socially responsible" and not just financial criteria. A portfolio of less than $125,000 would be extremely hard pressed to become properly diversified without the use of mutual funds, regardless of what some brokers and financial advisors will tell you.

Be extremely wary of the excessive costs involved in strategies that avoid mutual funds in smaller portfolios. I will stress again that most brokers and advisors are paid commissions and often push their individual stocks and bonds to smaller investors so they can enhance their own commissions, rather than addressing the needs of their clients. Brokers and commission-oriented financial planners sell mutual funds that usually have costs that can be up to four or five times higher than no-load/low-fee funds.

Because of their ability to pool the investment capital from thousands of different investors, mutual funds have a great ability to diversify, which significantly reduces risk. Of course, with billions of dollars under management (upon which to charge fees), most funds have top talent guiding their portfolios. Many of these managers specialize in growth, income, or total return funds, for example, and have several years' experience with the same fund. Other mutual funds, called index funds, are designed to do only as well as the stock market or some sort of investment index (such as the S&P 500 or Bond Index); they generally have very low fees.

As mentioned earlier, mutual funds – even those sold by nice, enlightened, socially conscious brokers and commission-oriented financial planners – usually have

". . .and Zen is nothing if not practical and grounded."

NORMAN FISCHER

much higher costs than no-load/low-fee funds. These high fees are often due to marketing costs which don't benefit the investor. Typically, these fees are charged as a front-end fee, up to 8.5% ($850 on a $10,000 investment), or they might catch you with back-end surrender fees, which serve as deferred sales charges. Funds that use these deferred/back-end loads/ back-end fees (whatever you prefer to call them) overcharge you on an annual basis in order to pay about 4% to their salespeople.

Using funds with front or back loads is unnecessary; similar, equally viable funds (without such costs) are available. You'll find a list of recommended socially responsible funds at the end of this chapter. All of them control their expenses and usually have fees that are significantly lower than those charged by their "loaded" counterparts.

Unfortunately, many financial institutions and financial planners are dumbing down their services by using mutual funds – exclusively – to build client portfolios. Some

firms charge up to 3% (if you add up the "hidden" mutual fund fees). Simply stated, you don't need to pay an advisor to select your mutual funds: do it yourself.

Realize that all mutual funds have fees and expenses. If you like the idea of someone doing your mutual fund portfolio for you, pay them a flat fee a year – no matter the size of your portfolio – for the peace of mind you might receive. Don't, don't, don't use a commissioned person to select any investments for you. Unless they are fee-only and experienced, don't use them. Your portfolio manager should be buying individual stocks and bonds, not just mutual funds for you. If they mainly use mutual funds, your portfolio is most likely being dumbed down to mediocre returns and excessive fees by a manager who is basically providing bookkeeping services.

You don't, of course, want to choose a fund simply because it has lower fees. By going directly to the mutual fund companies or using an investment manager, you can avoid paying high marketing fees to brokers and other commissioned professionals. Several funds specialize in working with money managers and educated investors who prefer going direct. Fund groups such as Vanguard, T. Rowe Price, Scudder, Stevens & Clark, SEI, Pimco, Schwab, Federated, et cetera, have all designed their products for individuals and professionals who make their decisions based on merit and careful analysis rather than the pressure tactics used by brokers. The problem remains, however, that these fund groups do not use any social criteria in managing portfolios. Also, be aware that a few so called "no-load" funds have loads on some of their portfolios.

Some load mutual funds have excellent management and a history of solid returns, to be sure. And if you presently own a load fund, it may make sense to keep it since you have already paid the front end fee. Some of my favorite load funds for transfer are Templeton, MFS, Sogen, Putnam, Franklin, American Funds, Calvert, and Fidelity.

When switching funds from Balanced or Stock funds in your Do-It-Yourself portfolio, always switch the fund with the smallest capital gain. Also, for taxable accounts, try to wait twelve to eighteen months before you switch in order to lower your tax liability (don't wait unless you are only a few months from a switch). If you have held a mutual fund for at least eighteen months, the capital gain rate is only 20%. If you have kept it for more than one year, but less than eighteen months, then the maximum rate is 28%. The same tax smart principles apply in the equity or balanced holdings of your tax-favored IRA, retirement, or pension accounts. For example, if you need to move $50,000 from stocks, and have sufficient funds to move it all from your IRA, do it from the tax-favored account to save taxes. Each portfolio doesn't need to be adjusted identically. Tax smart asset allocation is the key.

I often interview mutual fund managers to decipher exactly what their goals are. Who do they see as their customer? Is it the young, aggressive hotshot who wants quick returns, or a retired person

In loving the people and ruling the state, can you proceed without any purpose of action? In the opening and shutting of the gates of heaven, can you do so as a female bird? Intelligence reaches in every direction, can you appear to be without knowledge?

TAO TE CHING

investing for an ever-increasing income and capital pool? Do they have any of their own money (how much?) in the fund they are managing? Knowing details of how a fund manager operates allows me to feel comfortable in recommending the fund to clients. Obviously, this is difficult to do on your own, but be sure to read the prospectus of a fund to understand their goals and philosophies.

Mutual funds allow you to purchase and sell shares at the day's-end share price. They are very easy to sell and usually sold without cost (although some have back-end fees, as mentioned earlier, to be avoided if possible).

If you choose to purchase mutual fund shares through a discount broker, be prepared for the modest fee they will charge. It's debatable whether this fee is worth it, but I feel the convenience of having your account held at a discount brokerage, with the monthly statements they produce (which eases record keeping), outweighs the small cost.

Socially Responsible Mutual Funds

On the next page we list an extensive group of "Social Criteria Funds" (gathered in part for us by Lipper Analytical Services) for investors inclined to have a portfolio of 100% socially driven funds. There are no guarantees that these funds will invest in companies you feel are ethical, nor does it mean that they will not own companies you dislike. Also understand that other funds are not necessarily socially "unconscious" funds.

Source: Lipper Analytical Services

Social Values Mutual Funds

No more than 10% of your portfolio should be held in any one growth fund; 15% in any one balanced fund; or 20% in any one bond fund. Build your diversified portfolio by choosing (beginning with Group 1) from each group of the following list of funds.

Growth Funds

Group 1

Aquinas Equity Income   800.223.7010
Ariel Appreciation   800.292.7435
*Calvert Fund Strategy   800.368.2748
*Calvert Social Investment Equity   800.767.1729
Citizens Index Fund, Institutional   800.223.7010
Domini Social Equity   800.762.6814
Green Century Equity Fund   800.934.7338
MMA Praxis Growth   800.977.2947
Rightime Social Awareness   800.242.1421

Group 2

Ariel Growth   800.292.7435
Bridgeway Ultra Small Companies   800.661.3550
Calvert Capital Accumulation   800.368.2748
Citizens Emerging   800.223.7010
Delaware Group Quantum Fund A   800.523.4640
Dreyfus Third Century   800.554.4611
Parnassus Fund   800.999.3505
Parnassus Fund   800.999.3505

Group 3

American Trust Allegiance   800.385.7003*
Aquinas Equity 800.423.6369
Bridgeway Socially Responsible   800.661.3550

*Calvert Managed   800.368.2748
Citizens Index Fund   800.223.7010
DEVCAP   800.371.2855
Hudson Investors Fund   800.483.7664
Neuberger & Berman   800.877.9700
New Alternatives 800.423.8383
Pax World Growth Fund   800.767.1729
Security Social Awareness Fund   800.888.2461
Timothy Plan Institutional   800.846.7526
Citizens Index Fund, Retail   800.223.7010
Womens Equity Mutual Fund   415.547.9135

Balanced Funds

Group 1

Pax World Fund   800.767.1729

Group 2

Calvert Social Investment   800.368.2748
Green Century Balanced   800.934.7336

Group 3

Aquinas Balanced   800.423.6369
Parnassus   800.999.3505

Social Values Mutual Funds continued

Bond Funds

Group 1
Aquinas Fixed Income Bond   800.423.6369
MMA Praxis Intermediate 800.977.2947

Group 2
*Calvert Income 800.368.2748
Parnassus Fixed Income 800.999.3505

Group 3
Citizens Income Fund 800.223.7010
*Calvert Social Bond 800.368.2748

Group 4
Eclipse Ultra Short Term 800.872.2710

International Stock Funds

*Calvert World Value Intl. Equity   800.368.2748
Citizens Global Equity   800.223.7010

*Calvert Funds are Load funds, though some brokerage firms allow you to buy the funds no-load. Make sure you do not pay a load on Calvert Funds.

Gold & Natural Resource Funds

T. Rowe Price New Era   800.638.5660
Blanchard Precious Metals   800.829.3863
United Services World Gold 800.USFUNDS

Unique Funds

Amana Islamic Growth Fund (Growth)   800.728.8762
Amana Islamic Income Fund (Bond)   800.728.8762
America Asia Allocation Growth   703.356.3720
*Calvert New Africa (Growth)   800.368.2748
Cruelty Free Value   800.662.9992
Meyers Pride Value   800.410.3337
Total Return Utilities Fund   800.325.3539
Utilities Growth Fund   800.325.3539
Womens Equity Mutual Fund (Growth)   415.547.9135

For your personal Cash Management account, consider the following two funds: Calvert Social Money Market   800.368.2748
Citizens Working Assets Money Fund   800.223.7010

Reality

Your first step in constructing a Do-It-Yourself market cycle portfolio is to assess your risk tolerance. This will enable you to appropriately choose one of the following strategies.

"Aggressive" investors must be patient, allowing their strategy a twelve year time horizon due to the volatility of this investment class. Such a strategy should be adhered to for at least six years and be prepared to handle 35% volatility. This means, your $100,000 portfolio may lose $35,000, and you should not panic.

"Growth" investors need to invest with a ten year horizon (hold on at least five years) and prepare for a possible 30% fluctuation in assets.

"Balanced" investors also must abide by a ten year horizon. This strategy is subject to 25% volatility where a $100,000 portfolio could lose as much as $25,000. Most investors and even retirees would be wise to follow the guidelines set forth for the Balanced investor.

"Yield" investors only need a five year horizon, holding on for at least four years at a time. At 15% volatility, this strategy is appropriate for most retirees and investors who need income generated from their investments.

"Capital Preservationist" investors can expect only 5% volatility and need not work from any longer than a one year horizon. Anyone who doesn't fit in the aforementioned strategies should follow the Capital Preservation guidelines.

Once you have determined your risk tolerance and appropriate strategy, turn to the worksheets in the Investor Resources section at the back of the book. Before you can actually make allocations you must check out the current yield of the stock market in *The Wall Street Journal, Barrons* (Market Laboratory Section), *Investors Business Daily,* or www.zenvesting.com.

Next you'll need to chose a broker and begin calling mutual fund companies that we have listed to request their literature. And once your assets are available through your broker you can follow the appropriate worksheet to get invested. Remember to consult the current yields and responsibly decide upon a risk tolerance.

If you find yourself bogged down by the project, consult a fee-only financial advisor to guide you through the process.

Fame or integrity:
*   which is more important?*
Money or happiness:
*   which is more valuable?*
Success or failure:
*   which is more destructive?*

If you look to others for fulfillment,
you will never truly be fulfilled.
If your happiness depends on money,
you will never be happy with yourself.

Be content with what you have;
rejoice in the way things are.
When you realize there is nothing
lacking, the whole world
belongs to you.

TAO TE CHING

Discount Brokers

The sheer number of discount brokers, and the breadth of services they provide, has increased dramatically due to online and other forms of "broker-less" trading. Each excel in certain areas, and while this is a fairly extensive compilation, there are dozens not listed. **Commissions charged and minimum fees change often, due to the competitive nature of the industry. Call to verify, as figures listed below could have changed.**

	Charles Schwab 800.435.4000 .schwab.com	Fidelity 800.544.8666 .fidelity.com	Jack White 800.431.3500 .jackwhiteco.com	Vanguard 800.992.8327 .vanguard.com	Muriel Siebert 800.872.0711 .msiebert.com
Online Trading	yes	yes	yes	yes	yes
View Account Online	yes	yes	yes	yes	yes
Number of No Transaction Fee Mutual Funds	over 825	over 700	over 1,300	0	over 600
Minimum Transaction Fee Per Trade	($29.95 online) $39	($19.95 online) $38	($25 online) $33	$36.25	($25 online) $37.50
Fee Per $10,000 Mutual Fund Transaction	.7% of principle	unavail	$33	$35	$69.50
Annual Cost for IRA/Less than $5,000 Balance	$29	$24	$35	0	$30
24 hour trading	yes	yes	yes	yes	yes
Live broker hours	24 hours/7days	24 hours/7days	24 hours/7days	8-5:30 M-F	7:30-7:30 M-F
SIPC & Excess Insurance to $	$99 million	$100 million	$50 million	$25 million	$100 million
Cash Management Account— Checkbook, Visa/MC, Cost	checkbook visa/mc free	checkbook visa/mc free	checkbook visa/mc free	checkbook	checkbook $0 visa/mc $60
CMA Minimum Balance	$2,500	$10,000	$3,000	0	$5,000

Discount Brokers

	Bull & Bear 800.285.5232 .bullbear.com.	National Discount Brokers 800.417.7423 .ndb.com	AmericanExpress Financial Direct 800.297.7010 .americanexpress. com	Ameritrade 800.669.3900 .ameritrade.com	DLJ Direct 888.456.4355 .dljdirect.com
Online Trading	yes	yes	yes	yes	yes
View Account Online	yes	yes	yes	yes	yes
Number of No Transaction Fee Mutual Funds	over 1,000	over 500	over 200	0	600
Minimum Transaction Fee Per Trade	($19.95 online)	($14.95 online) $25	($24.95 online) $49	($8 online) $18	$20
Fee Per $10,000 Mutual Fund Trans	$48	$20	$0 for record-keeping, $40 for early redemption	$18	$35
Annual Cost for IRA/Less than $5,000 Balance	0	$35	$0	$0	$35
24 hour trading	yes	yes	yes	yes	yes
Live broker hours	8:30-5 M-F	7:30-830 M-F	7-12 M-F 9-6 S-S	6-10 M-F	7-1am M-F
SIPC & Excess Insurance to $	$50 million	$75 million	$25 million	$10.5 million	$50 million
Cash Management Account— Checkbook, Visa/MC, Cost	checkbook $0	checkbook visa/mc	checkbook visa/mc	no	checkbook visa/mc
CMA Minimum Balance	$5,000	0/$10,000	$0	$2,000	$0

DOLLAR COST AVERAGING THE DO-IT-YOURSELF WAY

4

If you make consistent monthly payments into a retirement account or long term savings program (5+ years), you are a prime candidate for this simple, effective strategy.

When starting out, the key is to make your payments into your most aggressive investments (no matter what the yield is on stocks), and then, on a quarterly basis, rebalance your portfolio in accordance with dividend yields. Beginning investors should dollar-cost-average into asset allocation funds or balanced funds from the list in the Sowing Seeds chapter, until you have over $5000. At that point, start to build a Do-It-Yourself portfolio described in the Sowing Seeds chapter.

What is the magic of dollar-cost-averaging? Simply time diversification and mathematics. Here is how it works. By committing a set amount of money into your mutual funds each month, the following happens: **see figure 4.1**

As you can see, dollar-cost-averaging won't guarantee you success in a falling market on a short term basis. Markets do tend to trend up over extended periods, so if you do find yourself investing into a falling market, you can celebrate because with each investment you are buying more shares.

401(k)s, TSAs, and other self directed retirement plans are especially well-suited for a program that incorporates the Do-It-Yourself strategy with a dollar-cost-averaging system. Although much of which will depend on the flexibility offered by your plan sponsor, the following rules apply:

4.1 Dollar Cost Averaging ($100 /month= $400 total)

MARKET	Sideways		Rising		Falling	
	Stock Price	# of shares	Stock Price	# of shares	Stock Price	# of shares
1st Month	$10	10	$10	10	$10	10
2nd Month	$9	11	$14	7	$7	14
3rd Month	$11	9	$20	5	$5	20
4th Month	$11	9	$25	4	$4	25
total shares		39		26		69

Sideways	Rising	Falling
39	26	69
x $11= $429	x $25= $650	x $4= $276
-$400	-$400	-$400
$29 gain	$250 gain	$124 loss

1. If you are only allowed to rebalance quarterly, check the stock yield ten days before you are able to switch. If yields suggest a change, do it then.
2. If you have only four rebalancing options a year, adhere to these two rules:
   a) if you are just getting started, rebalance quarterly;
   b) if your account value is over five times your annual deposits, rebalance as yields change. If you are running out of rebalancing options, use only 3% and 5% yield thresholds as triggers.
3. If you are allowed unlimited rebalancing options, and are making consistent deposits, rebalance at least quarterly. Otherwise, do so based on yield changes.
4. Use managed funds. Avoid indexed funds, if possible.
5. If no gold/natural resource funds, substitute international funds, and stock funds. If no stock funds, substitute balanced funds. If no balanced funds, substitute 50% stock/ 50% bonds.

Making Dollar Cost Averaging Work

Make a Commitment

To reap the rewards of the compounding interest phenomena, discipline yourself to set aside a certain amount monthly. Money and time work magic together; start early.

Determine Your Willingness for Risk

Aggressive – Growth – Balanced – Yield – Capital Preservation

Follow the Yield

You can find listings for the current dividend yields on both the Dow Jones and S&P 500 in business magazines such as *The Wall Street Journal, Barrons, Investors Business Daily,* or www.zenvesting.com.

Identify Your Investor Type

Use the worksheets on the following pages to decide an appropriate investment program based on your risk tolerance.

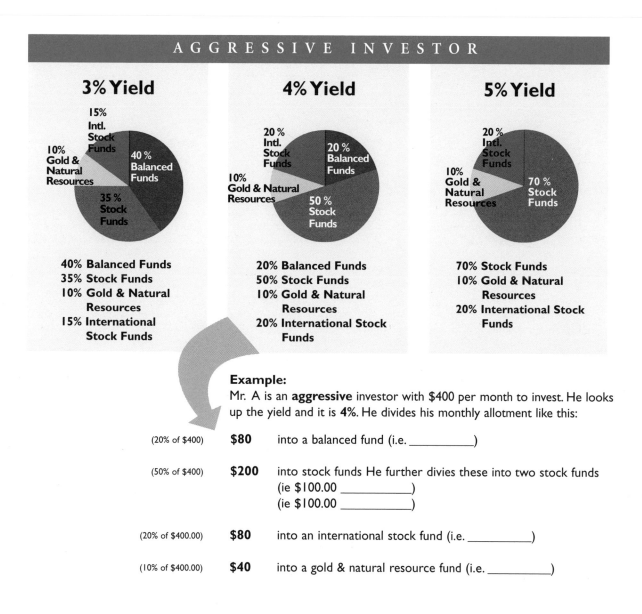

AGGRESSIVE INVESTOR

3% Yield

40% Balanced Funds
35% Stock Funds
10% Gold & Natural
Resources
15% International
Stock Funds

4% Yield

20% Balanced Funds
50% Stock Funds
10% Gold & Natural
Resources
20% International Stock
Funds

5% Yield

70% Stock Funds
10% Gold & Natural
Resources
20% International Stock
Funds

Example:

Mr. A is an **aggressive** investor with $400 per month to invest. He looks up the yield and it is **4%**. He divides his monthly allotment like this:

(20% of $400) **$80** into a balanced fund (i.e. _____)

(50% of $400) **$200** into stock funds He further divies these into two stock funds
(ie $100.00 _____)
(ie $100.00 _____)

(20% of $400.00) **$80** into an international stock fund (i.e. _____)

(10% of $400.00) **$40** into a gold & natural resource fund (i.e. _____)

GROWTH INVESTOR

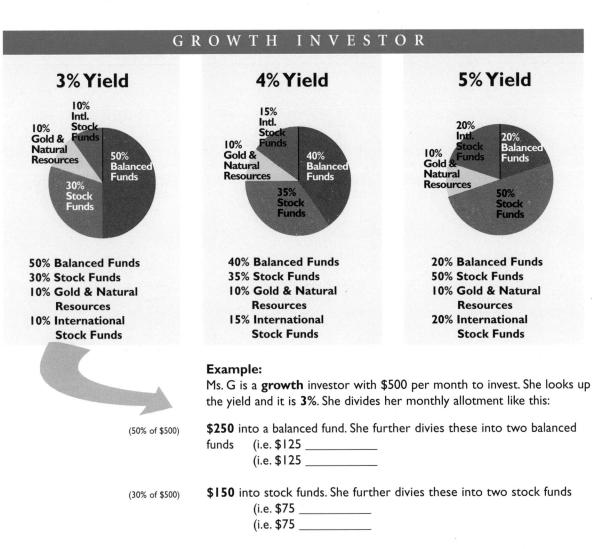

3% Yield

10% Intl. Stock Funds
10% Gold & Natural Resources
30% Stock Funds
50% Balanced Funds

50% Balanced Funds
30% Stock Funds
10% Gold & Natural Resources
10% International Stock Funds

4% Yield

15% Intl. Stock Funds
10% Gold & Natural Resources
35% Stock Funds
40% Balanced Funds

40% Balanced Funds
35% Stock Funds
10% Gold & Natural Resources
15% International Stock Funds

5% Yield

20% Intl. Stock Funds
10% Gold & Natural Resources
20% Balanced Funds
50% Stock Funds

20% Balanced Funds
50% Stock Funds
10% Gold & Natural Resources
20% International Stock Funds

Example:

Ms. G is a **growth** investor with $500 per month to invest. She looks up the yield and it is **3%**. She divides her monthly allotment like this:

(50% of $500) **$250** into a balanced fund. She further divies these into two balanced funds   (i.e. $125 _____
(i.e. $125 _____

(30% of $500) **$150** into stock funds. She further divies these into two stock funds
(i.e. $75 _____
(i.e. $75 _____

(10% of $500) **$50** into a gold and natural resources fund (i.e. _____)

(10% of $500) **$50** into an international fund (i.e. _____)

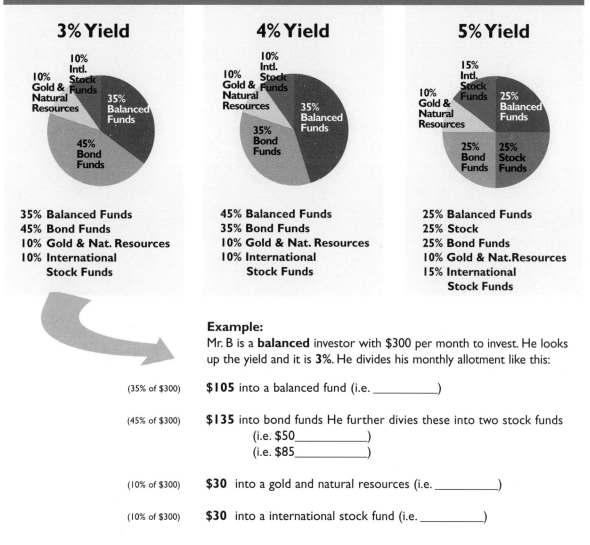

BALANCED INVESTOR

3% Yield

10% Intl. Stock Funds
10% Gold & Natural Resources
35% Balanced Funds
45% Bond Funds

35% Balanced Funds
45% Bond Funds
10% Gold & Nat. Resources
10% International
  Stock Funds

4% Yield

10% Intl. Stock Funds
10% Gold & Natural Resources
35% Balanced Funds
35% Bond Funds

45% Balanced Funds
35% Bond Funds
10% Gold & Nat. Resources
10% International
  Stock Funds

5% Yield

15% Intl. Stock Funds
10% Gold & Natural Resources
25% Balanced Funds
25% Bond Funds
25% Stock Funds

25% Balanced Funds
25% Stock
25% Bond Funds
10% Gold & Nat. Resources
15% International
  Stock Funds

Example:

Mr. B is a **balanced** investor with $300 per month to invest. He looks up the yield and it is **3%**. He divides his monthly allotment like this:

(35% of $300)   **$105** into a balanced fund (i.e. _____)

(45% of $300)   **$135** into bond funds He further divies these into two stock funds
  (i.e. $50_____)
  (i.e. $85_____)

(10% of $300)   **$30** into a gold and natural resources (i.e. _____)

(10% of $300)   **$30** into a international stock fund (i.e. _____)

YIELD INVESTOR

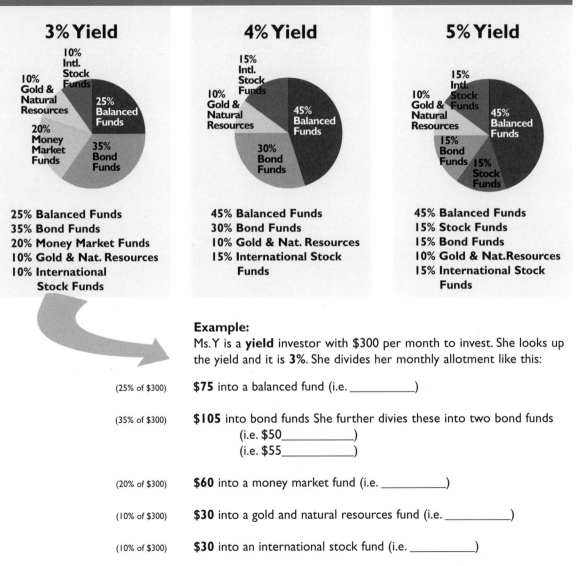

3% Yield

10% Intl. Stock Funds
10% Gold & Natural Resources
25% Balanced Funds
20% Money Market Funds
35% Bond Funds

25% Balanced Funds
35% Bond Funds
20% Money Market Funds
10% Gold & Nat. Resources
10% International
   Stock Funds

4% Yield

15% Intl. Stock Funds
10% Gold & Natural Resources
45% Balanced Funds
30% Bond Funds

45% Balanced Funds
30% Bond Funds
10% Gold & Nat. Resources
15% International Stock
   Funds

5% Yield

15% Intl. Stock Funds
10% Gold & Natural Resources
45% Balanced Funds
15% Bond Funds
15% Stock Funds

45% Balanced Funds
15% Stock Funds
15% Bond Funds
10% Gold & Nat.Resources
15% International Stock
   Funds

Example:

Ms. Y is a **yield** investor with $300 per month to invest. She looks up the yield and it is **3%**. She divides her monthly allotment like this:

(25% of $300)   **$75** into a balanced fund (i.e. _____)

(35% of $300)   **$105** into bond funds She further divies these into two bond funds
            (i.e. $50_____)
            (i.e. $55_____)

(20% of $300)   **$60** into a money market fund (i.e. _____)

(10% of $300)   **$30** into a gold and natural resources fund (i.e. _____)

(10% of $300)   **$30** into an international stock fund (i.e. _____)

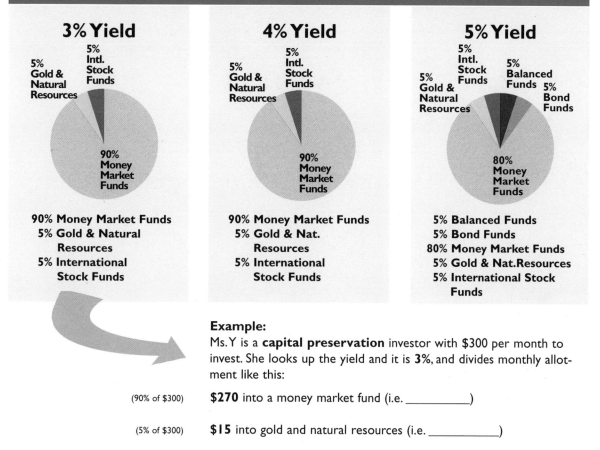

CAPITAL PRESERVATION INVESTOR

3% Yield

5% Gold & Natural Resources

5% Intl. Stock Funds

90% Money Market Funds

90% Money Market Funds
5% Gold & Natural Resources
5% International Stock Funds

4% Yield

5% Gold & Natural Resources

5% Intl. Stock Funds

90% Money Market Funds

90% Money Market Funds
5% Gold & Nat. Resources
5% International Stock Funds

5% Yield

5% Intl. Stock Funds

5% Gold & Natural Resources

5% Balanced Funds

5% Bond Funds

80% Money Market Funds

5% Balanced Funds
5% Bond Funds
80% Money Market Funds
5% Gold & Nat. Resources
5% International Stock Funds

Example:

Ms. Y is a **capital preservation** investor with $300 per month to invest. She looks up the yield and it is **3%**, and divides monthly allotment like this:

(90% of $300)   **$270** into a money market fund (i.e. _____)

(5% of $300)   **$15** into gold and natural resources (i.e. _____)

(5% of $300)   **$15** into a international stock fund (i.e. _____)

RELIEVING YOUR GUARDIAN ANGEL:
PROPER INSURANCE

5

Insurance is a means of reducing or limiting a risk by dividing the loss among many individuals. It is a powerful, effective tool when used judiciously. You should not insure against predictable risks whose financial effect would be modest, such as the potential need for new eyeglasses or a capped tooth. It is fiscally wise to only transfer risks which would be harmful to your financial well-being.

Deductibles and other cost-sharing methods greatly help reduce the cost of insurance while fulfilling its purpose. Note, for example, the tremendous savings in purchasing car insurance by accepting a $500 or $1,000 additional risk in the deductible.

Commissions, accounting, administration, marketing, and overhead expenses all are paid out of commissions, so understand that insurers can only give back a certain percentage of your premium. So if you can handle the $500 cost of replacing your car window, then choose a $500 deductible on your car insurance, and take advantage of the savings in premi-

ums. The point is, you need to worry about purchasing insurance for the $10,000, $100,000, or $1,000,000 calamities, not the small, incidental expenses. These small sums should be taken care of by setting aside a reserve fund.

A sad fact of the insurance industry is the conflict of interest caused by commissions paid to agents. Keep this in mind when they recommend a modest or no deductible policy which may cost $600 or $800 more than a $500 deductible on a similar policy. Of course, your agent sees a healthier commission on the higher premium.

Property & Liability Insurance

Buying property and liability insurance is vitally important to your financial security. When purchasing property insurance be aware of possible losses you might incur by ownership. Decide what type of insurance best covers your assumed risks, how much insurance you should carry, and finally, what company to choose for insurance coverage. Again, buy insurance only to cover substantial risk.

Complicated, ever-changing policies require locating an honest, expert insurance agent. If possible, choose one that is fee-only. Let them know initially that the policy should cover you only against the risks that are substantial, no matter how remote that risk. It is equally important to find out which risks the policy does not cover, and which are being transferred. You can, at that point, decide whether the risks you will be assuming are manageable. If not, transfer them to the insurance company.

Umbrella Liability Coverage

Use personal umbrella liability insurance to provide catastrophic coverage over the required underlying limit on home and auto policies (home and auto limits generally must be $300,000 but this varies by company). It also fills many cracks and loopholes and provides worldwide liability coverage, while home and auto policies alone do not.

Health Insurance

It is important that you, family members, and anyone that is dependent on you have a comprehensive, major medical policy covering reasonable hospital and medical expenses. Your policy should pay private or semi-private room charges, intensive care, and burn, or cardiac care unit expenses in full, for an unlimited number of days. It should also include a co-payment and per year stop loss provision at an amount you can handle out-of-pocket. The policy should cover pre-existing conditions and have a maximum limit of no less than $500,000 ($1,000,000 is more reasonable). Cancellation protection should also be provided by the policy's contract.

As with all insurance policies, it is always wise to ask your insurance advisor for a list of the limitations of your policy and charges your policy will not cover. Standard policy exclusions would be war, self-inflicted injuries, medical expenses that had no costs, expenses covered by a V.A. hospital, et cetera.

KEY PROVISIONS A HEALTH INSURANCE POLICY SHOULD HAVE:

1. Reasonable and customary coverage of hospital and medical expenses.
2. Full semi-private room coverage.
3. Full intensive care, burn unit, cardiac care coverage to policy maximum – not for certain number of days.
4. Per year payment and Stop/Loss Provisions at whatever level you feel you can handle, i.e., $1,000, $5,000, $100,000, et cetera.
5. Full coverage of pre-existing conditions.
6. A minimum policy limit of $500,000, although $1,000,000 is much better.
7. Cancellation protection.

Life Insurance

As you accept more responsibility and obligation in life, you will find it important to provide your dependents with economic security and financial well-being in case you die. In most cases, your family will need the income produced by wealth, and not just assets. While some insurance agents would like you to think that everyone needs life insurance, you only need this form of insurance if someone would suffer financially as a consequence of your death. Therefore, your need for life insurance is probably nonexistent if you are single and no one is dependent on you. Likewise, if you have a substantial net worth, and your death would not cause economic havoc in anyone's life (because you have already built up a sizable nest egg), life insurance is unnecessary. **Figure 5.1** is a worksheet that can help you determine whether or not you need life insurance.

Many people go wrong, however, by looking only at a specific amount of death benefit, rather than what the death benefit will provide in monthly income. Income is the key. It is not the amount of assets, but the purchasing power those assets can generate.

Over time, inflation will destroy the value of any income stream that is not structured to offset a rising cost of living. In order to ensure

5.1 Life Insurance Worksheet

STEP 1

List below who would suffer financially if you died. (Example: spouse, children, parents, business partners, charity, friends, siblings.)

Name   List type of loss (i.e., income, debt payback, family care, and so on)

_____

_____

_____

_____

STEP 2

List a specific amount of economic support for the above listed people.

Monthly income to   _____   of $ _____

Monthly income to   _____   of $ _____

Pay off debts of $ _____   for   _____

Cash resource of $ _____   for   _____

Special cash to   _____   of $ _____ lump sum.

STEP 3

Total monthly income desired @ $_____ divided by 0.005 = $ _____

Total cash needed to pay off debts, mortgages, for cash reserves, and special cash = $ _____

Total assets needed to provide for above = $ _____
(A 6% interest rate is used so that excess earnings can go to help offset inflation.)

Total assets needed (from above) $ _____

Less liquid assets you own and assets that could be made liquid $ _____

Total insurance death benefit you need $ _____

that your dependent's income will go up annually, assume that your assets will only earn a 6% return; your assets should hopefully earn more than 6%, allowing them a raise every year, and helping to offset inflation.

For example, if $100,000 earned 12% in the first year ($112,000), your dependents would receive (at a 6% payout, with the balance reinvested) $500 monthly, or $6,000 annual income. In addition, the $100,000 would have grown to $106,000. The following year, assuming a 12% return and 6% payout, the $106,000 would generate $530 a month (or $6,360 a year). These annual increases in cash flow should help keep pace with inflation.

Make it a habit to check your insurance coverage amount often. The checklist (**Figure 5.2**) should help you realize when you need to review your insurance. Since it is unnecessary to pay for a benefit you don't need, you should decrease the amount of insurance you own as your net worth increases.

A competent estate planning attorney can assist you in setting up the proper trusts and will arrangements so that your life insurance program is coordinated with your estate plan. To further ensure life insurance income to a dependent, it is probably best to have your insurance proceeds paid directly to a trust, which will then provide income on a monthly basis.

Who Else to Insure

In addition to the insurance on *your* life, there are other people you might also insure, such as a spouse, especially if he or she stays at home to take care of the children. High quality daycare is extremely important and expensive. Should you lose your spouse, you will need to hire someone to fulfill those childcare responsibilities.

You might consider purchasing insurance to ensure your business partner's economic stability should you die. For example, your partner might have to purchase your interest in a partnership arrangement you have with other investors. Also, consider organizations such as charities

"Love, compassion, joy and equanimity are the very nature of an enlightened person. They are the four aspects of true love within ourselves and within everyone and everything."

THICH NHAT HANH

5.2 Death Benefit Insurance Checklist

Check your insurance coverage amount:

- The day you or your spouse becomes pregnant.
- If your debt structure changes – you take on a new debt or pay off an old one.
- If you get married.
- If someone becomes dependent on you (parent, child, sibling).
- If your net worth increases by $25,000 or more.
- If you change jobs, take on a partner, change business form (incorporate).
- If you have not reviewed your insurance within 12 to 18 months.

to which you donate services or money.

Do not waste insurance premiums to purchase a substantial amount of life insurance on your children. The primary need for insurance on children is to provide them with the guaranteed right to buy more insurance when they get older, should they become uninsurable.

Pricing

Three things affect the pricing of an insurance policy. First, the cost of the risk. For example, what are the chances of your dying? This is often called the mortality cost, pure term cost, or pure insurance expense by the insurance company. The next element of cost is the earnings on the investments of the insurance company. Third is the administrative expense, inherent in writing an insurance policy – taxes, agent commissions, printing costs, billing costs, advertising expenses, and so on.

Under no circumstances should you use your life insurance policy as a capital accumulator. Do your capital accumulating through your pension or profit-sharing plan, IRAs, TSAs, 401(k)s, et cetera. A handful of very large insurance companies were fined severely for marketing life insurance policies as investments.

When considering a life insurance policy, try to purchase one that will have the lowest cost over the period you own the policy, and in order to maximize your savings, purchase term insurance from a fee-only advisor or directly from a company.

Consider purchasing 5 to 20 year term policies through a no/

5.3 Sample Term Insurance Rates

$500,000 **No Commission** **Guaranteed annually** **renewable & convertible** **Annual term premium**	$370	$375	$385	$450	$565	$965	$2,825
$500,000 **No Commission** **5 year level term premium**	$385	$390	$420	$530	$720	$1,550	$3,810
$500,000 **No Commission** **10 year level term premium**	$385	$395	$435	$590	$810	$1,775	$4,670
$500,000 **No Commission** **20 year level term premium**	$525	$570	$680	$930	$1,390	$3,205	NA
AGE	25	30	35	40	45	55	65

low commission company like Ameritas (800.745.6665), USAA (800.531.8000), or Schwab Insurance Direct (800.838.0650) and always buy as much insurance death benefit as you need. Never jeopardize your family's financial security to save a few dollars.

Rules for Life Insurance

Never purchase decreasing term insurance. It generally costs more than other forms of term insurance and does not give you the option of leaving your policy at a level death benefit, should your net worth not increase as much as planned. There are many insurance products that benefit both agent and insurance company at the expense of the policyholder. These policies are sometimes called deposit term or modified premium term, both of which require a high initial contribution to the policy. Once you decide how

The Tao produces all things and nourishes them; it produces them and does not claim them as its own; it does all, and yet does not boast of it; it presides over all, and yet does not control them. This is what is called the mysterious quality of the Tao.

TAO TE CHING

much insurance death benefit you need and compare the alternatives, usually you'll find that deposit term or modified premium term is not the best value. Other products to avoid are load whole life, universal, variable life, second to die, or single premium policies. They are counterproductive when building an efficient financial and insurance program.

The following rules should help guide you in your purchase:

1. Buy only as much life insurance as you really need, and only if you need it.If your needs will decrease over the years as your net worth grows, make sure you're buying insurance designed to have good low net cost.

2. Make sure each policy's ownership and beneficiary designation is consistent with your current financial situation and your estate plan. Most agents are just plain sloppy about their beneficiary designations. Improperly configured policies can cause unnecessary estate tax consequences.

3. Choose only companies rated A or A+ by A.M. Best, or in the top few rating classes by Moody's, Standard & Poor's, or Duff & Phelps.

4. If you need more than $500,000 of insurance, diversify. For $500,000 to $2,000,000 of coverage, use two companies; for over $2,000,000, divide your coverage among three companies. Again, if you use only one company, stick to a company rated A+ by A.M. Best, and one rated in one of the highest categories by Moody's, Standard & Poor's, or Duff & Phelps.

5. Get your life insurance advice from an objective fee-only financial planner, or a fee-only insurance consultant. Pay up to $300 an hour for good, objective advice; a good planner, however, should require only a few hours. Be sure to have everything in writing, and make sure the advice fits perfectly.

6. Use low-load policies, purchased without any agents

commission or marketing costs, through a fee-only life insurance counselor. A fee insurance agent charges a flat rate for assistance in analyzing and choosing your coverage, rather than a typical agent, who does it for free, but usually gets a high commission for advice.

If you do your insurance yourself, USAA (800.531.8000), Ameritas (800.745.6665) or Schwab (800.838.0650) can help you decide how much you need and your best beneficiary/ownership designations. Your lawyer or financial planner can also help.

7. Review your insurance annually at the very least, or when your financial or personal life changes. As specified earlier, reexamine and, if needed, increase your insurance coverage when you marry, have children, or take on debt. Consider reducing coverage as your net worth grows, children leave home, and debts are paid off.

8. If you or your adviser find that term insurance is the best product for you, choose a one to ten year term, guaranteed renewable to age 65 (or 25 years). Choose a policy that can be converted by a contract guarantee to a low-load cash value policy at any time before you reach age 65 (or 25 years).

9. If you are one of those rare people who wants a cash value policy, such as universal life, or adjustable life, carefully review the cash values in years one through five. Buy only a low-load policy (unless your spouse is a commissioned life insurance agent).

Income Protection Insurance

The most important insurance a working person can purchase is income protection, or disability insurance. Imagine yourself as a money machine and your primary assets are your skills and your ability to utilize them. If you are debilitated through sickness or accident, the effect on your financial security would be tremendous. Thus, it is very important to understand what your insurance provides if you're disabled, and even more important, to understand how your insurance company defines disabled. A standing joke among insurance agents is that some disability policies are written with such tight restrictions that if you could sell pencils on a street corner, you would not be considered disabled.

Figure 5.4 may be utilized to help you decide how much disability income insurance you will need to support your lifestyle (unless you have extensive personal assets that negates the need for disability insurance), and also help you decide what elimination period you should have on your policy.

An elimination period is the number of days you must wait before you receive a benefit from your policy. Generally it runs from a 30-days – substantially more expensive – to a two-year wait.

Key contract provisions you should have in your policy are outlined in **Figure 5.5**. In addition to the contract provisions listed,

another way to structure your policy is a graded or step premium policy which keeps your premiums low for a few years, then gradually increases until the premium levels off after a certain period. These policies are an excellent buy.

Love & Commitment

My then fifteen year old brother-in-law made one of those very difficult phone calls to me several years ago, just minutes after my father died after a yearlong battle with adrenal cancer. I reassured him that we all had been expecting it because two days earlier the doctor announced that death could come at any time. Of course, the news was still a shock. My thoughts went instantly to my mother who still had four of my siblings at home. I was comforted by the knowledge that she didn't need to worry about finances. Dad's disability insurance paid the mortgage and other bills while he fought for a year. His top quality medical insurance paid all but a couple hundred dollars of his sixty thousand dollar medical bill.

So, unlike some families who are devastated by the disability of a breadwinner, we were able to concentrate on healing, loving, and supporting dad and each other through the illness. His insurance policies paid off the mortgage, debts, and provided mom with a nest egg, as well as a less stressful work schedule.

Mom also did not have to worry about probate or inflexible court ordered asset protection rules because they had done some estate planning. And while they weren't rich – he never made more than $40,000 and she $20,000 – they had planned and that was a godsend.

Today insurance planning is much less expensive and easier than ever. Many employers have disability insurance, group life insurance, and hospital medical to build a solid insurance plan from.

Otherwise call 800.745.6665 to reach Ameritas, 800.531.8000 for USAA, or 800.838.0650 to talk to Schwab Insurance Direct for

5.4 Disability Income Insurance Worksheet

A. Amount of monthly income you need to support your lifestyle
(debt payments, utilities, food, entertainment, education, et cetera)? $ _____

B. Current investments which could be quickly converted to cash? $ _____

   Divided by monthly income needed: $ _____

   Equals number of months personal funds will support you: _____

C. Income expected should you become disabled:

   1st month $_____ 2nd month $_____ 3rd month $ _____

Elimination Period Calculation

Number of months receivables will support you: _____

Number of months liquid investments will support you: _____

Equals the elimination period in months: _____

Income needed to support your lifestyle: $ _____

Subtract income from assets not figured in liquidity analysis
such as Pension Plan assets, IRA, Income Partnerships, et cetera;
multiply value of these assets by .005 = $ _____
(For example, $1,000,000 x .005 = $5,000 monthly).
Amount of income needed from disability income insurance: $ _____

Note: Benefit period should always be at least to age 65 for sickness or accident, and usually lifetime for both sickness and accident.

inexpensive quotes for good low cost term insurance. A competent lawyer and insurance agent can help with the rest.

In my father's case, the insurance policies and solid estate planning was truly the most considerate love letter he wrote to his family. His actions showed his love and commitment.

5.5 Key Contract Provisions

Important Contract Provision	Benefit and Importance of Provision
1. Payment at age 65 or Lifetime benefit, if possible.	Pays you at least to age 65, to provide long term security.
2. Favorable definition of disability, regarding either: 1) "Your Occupation" or 2) "With Residual."	**"Your Occupation"** definition protects your ability to earn a living doing what you do now. This policy will pay you even if you work in another profession. **"With Residual"** benefit provides a benefit tied to either earnings lost or percent of time spent at occupation lost due to disability. A benefit based on earnings lost is far superior to time lost and should always be purchased. In fact, an "earnings lost" residual policy is better than a "your occupation" policy. Some policies pay full benefits even if you earn up to 49% of your pre-disability pay.
3. Cost of Living/Inflation Protection benefit.	Post disability benefits can increase with inflation, i.e., price increases. This provision is very important. Minimum increase you should purchase is 6% a year up to three times policy benefit (current benefit of $4,000 monthly could raise to $12,000 monthly maximum). Some policies increase benefits regardless of inflation rate.
4. Non-cancelable/guaranteed renewable coverage.	Policy cannot be changed by anyone except you. Premiums are guaranteed not to increase above level stated in policy.
5. Subsequent Disability Reoccurrence provision.	Waives a new elimination period if, following a disability, you become disabled again from the same or another cause.
6. Earnings definition should include pension contributions and all bonuses.	Helps assure you will get residual benefit.
7. Pre-existing conditions covered if listed on policy application.	Some policies only cover sickness or accidents first "manifest" while policy is in force, i.e., supposing you had back problems in high school, company could deny claim based on injury prior to buying policy.

Note: Your Disability Income Insurance Policy is the most important insurance you can own. Make sure your policy fits your needs completely and has no loopholes.

5.6 Disability Letter

Dear Disability Carrier:

I have the following questions regarding my policy:

1. What is your definition of disability?
2. If I were unable to perform my job, would I be disabled?
3. If I am only partially disabled, does it give me a benefit?
4. If I am partially disabled and working half-time, does it give me a benefit? If so, how much and for how long?
5. If I am partially disabled and earn one-half of what I earned prior to disability, what would my benefit be?
6. If I had a heart attack and was out of work for one year, started working again but only worked half days, would you pay me? If so, how much and for how long?
7. If I were disabled by a heart attack for a period of 3 years, then went back to work full time, most of my clients would have found other professionals to handle their needs. Would you pay me (while I was working full time) a benefit while rebuilding my practice? If you would pay me a benefit, what would that benefit be and for how long?
8. Is this policy cancelable by you?
9. Are my premium rates guaranteed never to go up?
10. Does this policy pay a dividend?
11. Does this policy cover conditions existing prior to my taking out the policy?
12. Does my policy have any waivers on it? If so, why?
13. What is my current elimination period, and can I change it?
14. Is there a waiver of premium benefit on my policy?
15. If I were disabled and collected benefits for 6 months, then went back to work for 6 months, before becoming disabled again, would I have to satisfy a new elimination period?
16. Does this policy have a presumptive disability benefit that pays me if I lose my sight, hearing, etc., even if I continue to work?
17. What is my policy's benefit period?
18. Can my policy's benefit period be changed to a lifetime sickness/lifetime accident benefit? If so, at what cost?
19. Does my policy have a cost of living benefit that raises my benefit as the Consumer Price Index rises? Can I add this benefit? At what cost?
20. I have lost my policy. Please send me forms to request a duplicate policy.
21. When was the last premium paid on this policy? When is the next due, and how much?
22. Does your policy offer a non-smoker discount?
23. Is my policy a participating dividend paying policy? If so, what dividends do you project? (I understand that dividends are not guaranteed.)
24. I am now in a group practice. Does your company have a group billing discount?
25. Who is the owner on this policy?
26. Who is the beneficiary?

Please send me the above information in writing, and thank you for your prompt attention.

Sincerely,

5.7 Inflation's Effect on Purchasing Power of Disability Insurance

Dollars required in the future to equal $1,000 in today's purchasing power at various rates of inflation.

% INFLATION	END OF YEAR 5	10	15	20	25
10%	$1,610	$2,590	$4,171	$6,730	$10,830
8%	$1,470	$2,160	$3,170	$4,660	$6,850
6%	$1,340	$1,790	$2,400	$3,200	$4,290
4%	$1,220	$1,480	$1,800	$2,190	$2,680

The state of vacancy should be brought to the highest degree, and that of stillness guarded with unwearying vigor. All things go through their processes of activity, then return to their original state. The vegetable world displays luxuriant growth, only to return to root. This returning is what we call the state of stillness, and that stillness may be called a fulfillment of an appointed end.

The report of that fulfilment is the regular, unchanging rule. To know this is to be intelligent, but not to leads to wild and evil issues. The unchanging rule leads to forbearance and a feeling of community with all things. From this comes a kingliness of character; and the one who is king-like goes on to be heaven-like. In that likeness to heaven you will have finally possessed the Tao endure a long life, exempt from all danger of decay.

TAO TE CHING

6

WE ALL DIE:
WE DON'T
KNOW WHEN

In Buddhism there are two certainties: we will die and secondly, we have no idea when our death will happen. This belief, and the understanding that we should not fret about what we can't control, has been a source of great comfort to Buddhists for thousands of years. In the course of a long (hopefully), full life, one usually acquires assets that can be thought of as a legacy to be passed on to family or friends. In fact, many of our relationships with family, friends, and business acquaintances have a financial component that exists even after death. Estate planning only benefits someone else, truly making it unusually spiritual at its very core.

Even so, this act of benevolence requires a bit more forethought than might be expected. Estate planning is the form in which you assign title to those assets. The <u>form</u> of ownership determines what happens to those assets in the event of your death (a court of law will decide if you don't).

In approaching an intentional estate plan there are five general questions to answer:

1. What is your estate and who owns it?
2. What are your objectives? *i.e., $ to family, help friends, start a foundation, security for children...*
3. What is your present estate plan?
4. Which of the available tools will best accomplish your objectives?
5. Who is responsible for keeping your estate plan current?

A typical estate consists of some or all of the following assets: Home, other real estate, furnishings and personal property, vehicles and recreational equipment, cash, checking and savings accounts, stocks and bonds, insurance, retirement plans, mortgages, notes land contracts.

Each of the above items – if owned by you – comprises your estate. If they are owned jointly, they are still part of your estate for tax, but not for probate purposes.

The first step in preparing

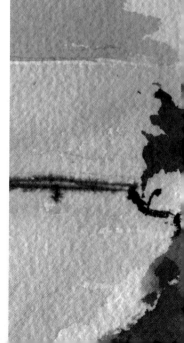

"All the teachings of the Buddha can be summed up in one word - Dharma. It means truth, that which really is. It also means law, the law which exists in a man's own heart and mind. It is the principle of righteousness."

U THITTILA

6.1 Estate Asset and Value Schedule

List property "item" in order of value: real estate, vehicles, household furnishings, jewelry, bank accounts, stocks, bonds, business interests, et cetera. These items comprise your estate.

Item	Market Value	Original Cost	Location	Ownership

your estate plan, is to make a list of your assets with values and ownership. This can be done with the help of an asset schedule – such as the one in **Figure 6.1,** and serves as the starting point of an estate planning discussion with your advisors. It will also constitute a permanent inventory of your estate that can be updated and reviewed as it changes.

After you have determined what your estate consists of you must decide your objectives, four of which are listed below:

1. Creating and conserving the estate for the benefit of your family or friends.
2. Providing orderly disposition of those assets to whom you wish them to go.
3. Reducing taxes and costs to a minimum.
4. Arranging for management of estate by a competent personal representative/trustee for the ease of your beneficiaries.

In addition to the type of estate, size of estate, and specific needs or desires of your family, friends, and charitable intentions, there will be other factors influencing your decision. It is vital that you review these items in detail.

Figures **6.2** and **6.3** illustrate specific estates and sample simplified estate plans. These sample estate plans work best as an educational tool to help you get a feel for planning strategies. After you have decided on your objectives and reviewed your estate with an advisor, determine what your present estate plan consists of. This might be a will and/or trust, or it simply may consist of insurance and the form of ownership in which you hold your assets. For instance, the law of your state may provide that assets you hold as joint tenant, with full rights of survivorship upon your death, will pass automatically to the other joint owner. On the other hand, if you hold title to the real estate as tenants in common, rather than as joint tenants, with full right of survivorship, your interest in that asset will be a part of your estate rather than passing

6.2 Sample Simplified Estate Plan

Kim and Gerry
age 35 and 36
1 child, 1 child on the way

CURRENT SITUATION

$ 2,500 IRA
$450,000 Home & Personal Assets
$400,000 Debts
$250,000 Insurance

GOALS:

- Income to spouse @ $5,000 monthly
- Debts paid
- Educate children (out of monthly income)
- Save estate and death costs

RECOMMENDATIONS

- Create will naming guardians for children, designating debts to be paid and assets to pass on to surviving spouse or children – in trusts.

- Name spouse as beneficiary of IRA; children as contingent beneficiaries.

- Raise insurance death benefits to $1,550,000 (to be used, as outlined below, at Kim's death).

DISTRIBUTION OF DEATH INSURANCE BENEFIT

- $950,000 outright to spouses' trust.
- $400,000 covering debts, and $50,000 for liquidity.
- $400,000 to provide income to spouse and children @ 6% = $2,000 monthly.
- $600,000 to family trust benefitting spouse and children @ $3,000 monthly.

Income to family for health, maintenance, educations, and support at approximately $5,000 per month (and debts paid off).

6.3 Sample Simplified Estate Plan

Page and Lee,
age 58 and 55
5 children, ages 22 through 30

CURRENT SITUATION
$1,400,000 IRA & Pension
$800,000 Home with $450,000 Mortgage
$300,000 Condo in Vail
$150,000 Group Life Insurance
$250,000 Personal Assets and Auto
Youngest Son Lives at Home

GOALS:
- Fully retire at age 65 with $10,000 monthly income.
- Provide lifetime income of $10,000 monthly to spouse if Page dies and pay off $450,000 mortgage.
- Provide lifetime income and support, if needed, to youngest son who struggles with depression and stress.
- Help grandchildren with incentives to go to college @ $25,000 each.
- Give each child $100,000 in cash. Balance of estate to charities.

RECOMMENDATIONS
- Purchase $900,000 of term insurance on Page to pay off debts and supplement IRA and pension income to Lee.
- Set up living trusts to maximize use of marital deductions (currently $600,000, rising to $1,000,000), avoid probate, and add confidentiality trusts to beneficiaries on new and group life insurance to maximize use of marital deductions.
- Trust to have provisions once Page and Lee have passed away to provide for youngest son (if needed) as first priority at up to $2,000 monthly income, hospital medical costs, and counseling expenses. Trustees to budget up to $4,000 monthly for this contingency and ear-mark $800,000 of estate assets to provide for his care. At youngest son's death, $800,000 to go to establish foundation of charities as directed by grandchildren.

- $100,000 paid to each child as lump sum.
- $25,000 set aside for each grandchild to be earmarked "paid to each grandchild once four year degree is earned."
- If there are additional funds, trustees at their discretion are to pay $25,000 additional for master's degree, and $25,000 for Ph.D.
- Remaining funds in trust fully dispersed to establish a foundation of charities as directed by grandchildren.
- IRA and pension beneficiaries to be Lee as primary and contingent in a manner consistent with the minimization of estate and income taxes and the goals of Page and Lee.

Note: Youngest son to have use of Page and Lee's home during his lifetime.
  *All numbers to be adjusted by inflation in constant 1998 dollars.

on to the other co-owner. These and other stipulations of law depend upon individual states and need to be reviewed accordingly with your advisors.

Another facet of your present estate plan that may have been created without intentional planning is the beneficiary designations on your life insurance. Promptly review your life insurance beneficiary and the amount of coverage with your advisors. You should reassess these decisions on a regular basis. Remember that the designation of beneficiaries and policy ownership can have estate and tax consequences.

It is important to analyze any changes in your estate or family situation that may require changes in your present plan. If you do not have a will, trust, or other estate planning documents, you nevertheless have an estate plan that can be referred to as the "state" plan. State law determines who will receive assets of someone who dies "intestate," or without a will. Since this law is inflexible and written to apply to general situations, it does not take into consid-

eration any special circumstances involving your estate and/or family situation. Of course, it is important to avoid the application of this law. Estate planning is a critical element of good financial planning; being aware and responsible ensures problems will be avoided in the future.

Once you have determined what your estate consists of, what your estate planning objectives are, and the laws applicable to your estate should you not plan, you can then review the available estate planning tools that might best accomplish your wishes. Naturally you should prepare your family for your death. If you follow the guidelines of **Figure 6.4,** your family should be able to return to financial normalcy after your death.

Wills, Trusts, and Other Estate Planning Tools

A will is a document which contains directions for the administration and disposition of your estate following your death by

"Am I my brother's keeper."

GENESIS 4:9

6.4 Estate Planning List

1. Your spouse (or father, mother, siblings, children, friends, et cetera), should know whom to call if you die, and where to find a list of your assets and important papers.

2. Your spouse should have a letter of instructions and suggestions of whom you feel should be trusted as an advisor for:
   a. Accounting
   b. Legal work
   c. Investment advice
   d. Insurance
   e. General financial planning help

3. Your spouse should know your specific wishes concerning funeral details, including: cremation, burial, organ gifting, and cemetery choice.

4. Your children should know whom you have named as guardians and why you chose those particular people.

5. You should have a "Letter of Values" written to your chosen guardians, stating why you picked them to care for your children. In addition, the letter should state your child rearing values, and beliefs on schooling, sports, colleges, summer camps, driving, travel, visiting relatives, et cetera. (A similar letter should go to your trustees.)

administration through Probate Court. A will must be prepared according to applicable state law. It does not enable a person to avoid probate, but enables a person to set forth their wishes as to how the estate will be probated, and to whom and when that estate will be distributed. Probate is the process that ensures that the wishes expressed in the will are carried out. The act of having a will prepared for you (and signing it) means you are, not during your lifetime, restricted in terms of the ownership, administration, or disposition of any of the assets that you own. Your will, though valid if prepared according to applicable state law, does not become effective until your death.

A trust is a separate legal entity created by means of a trust document, either separately or as a part of your will. The trust may be in the form of a "testamentary" trust that is included as part of your will, and comes into existence following your death and after the probate of your estate. Trusts may also take the form of a living trust, sometimes referred to as a revocable living (or loving) trust, which is a separate document from your will and is funded during your lifetime.

The revocable living trust is entirely revocable during your lifetime, to the extent that it is funded with your assets during your lifetime. The assets in the trust will not be probated at the time of your death because the trust is a separate legal entity and its existence continues after your death. A living trust allows you control over the trust assets and administration; you can name yourself as trustee and administer the trust assets during your lifetime, with a successor trustee named in the document to take over the administration of the trust assets immediately upon your death.

The trust can also be used to reduce estate taxes by dividing your estate following your death into separate shares for surviving spouse, children, friends (family and marital trusts).

The trust, whether a living trust or a testamentary trust, may

Knowing others is intelligence; knowing yourself is true wisdom. Mastering others is strength; mastering yourself is true power.

If you realize that you have enough, you are truly rich. If you stay in the center and embrace death with your whole heart, you will endure forever.

TAO TE CHING

be designed simply for the purpose of receiving insurance proceeds following your death. In addition, it might contain the directions for administration and distribution of those proceeds, with no other assets intended as trust funding.

An irrevocable trust may be appropriate if one of your objectives is to remove assets from your estate for the benefit of other beneficiaries without an immediate outright distribution to those beneficiaries. You may also accomplish estate reduction by means of gifts. If these gifts are less than $10,000 per donee, they will not incur a gift tax. If the gifts are to charitable, religious, educational, or similar organizations, they may qualify for the income tax charitable deduction. Such trusts are not usually subject to an amount limitation.

Another important estate planning tool is Durable Power of Attorney. This is a document wherein you designate someone as your "attorney-in-fact" and give them limited or broad powers to handle your business affairs, including making personal decisions for you in the event of your incompetency. It is valid only during your lifetime. Any such authority granted in that document terminates upon your death. It can allow you to avoid the involvement of a probate court in the establishment of a guardianship or conservatorship to supervise the administration of your estate or personal decisions during your period of incompetency.

In addition to preparing for death in legal terms, prepare your loved ones emotionally. Write a letter to "key players" outlining your wishes, and how they are to be carried out. The argument exists that estate planning is a grand preparation for something that – least of all – benefits the planner, so why do it at all? Life and love is also a preparation. After eighty or so years of magnificent pleasures and dreadful heartbreaks, death does seem a bit anticlimatic. Your memory will be noted by how you positively or negatively influenced the people around you.

Values

What are your values? If you die with fifty cents or fifty million dollars, what legacy do you wish to leave? It is a tragedy that so many estate plans represent the values of the attorney drafting the wills and trusts, with not nearly enough input from the client.

I remember being involved in a family meeting with a client's children to disclose that upon their parents' death, each of them would inherit enough money to significantly change their behavior. The parent's goal at the family meeting was to tell the kids to relax, and to quit worrying about retirement and saving for the education of their children because they would inherit enough to provide for their needs.

One of the daughters said "I've been losing sleep over whether to set aside $25 a week for retirement or send Cassidy to singing lessons."

Another remarked "my gosh, I've been wrestling with an after school latch key arrangement so that we can save for a college fund. Instead I would love to quit my second job so that I could be home to meet them when they get off the bus." The grateful daughter's eyes then filled with tears and hugs abounded.

Finally we then talked about a portion of the estate that would be taxed at 66% unless the children all agreed to choose a charity. The parents purposely opted out of this conversation but were proud to see their offspring excitedly spend two hours discussing a long list of social ills they might positively influence with a donation.

A WORD ON CHOICE OF GUARDIANS

For a couple with small children the most important estate planning decision is who to name as guardians. This can be a very difficult decision. Ideally, you want a stable couple who share your values and love your children as much as you do. Your family or friends have often built relationships with your children, and you have been able to watch them parent their children. In this way you can get a feel for their philosophy and values. It is entirely appropriate for you to sit down and ask them if they would be willing to be named guardians of your children and to also name the constraints with which you would want your children raised.

For example, my wife and I do not believe in physical punishment and made the conscious decision that if we were going to err on the side of being too lenient or too strict, we would err on the side of leniency. In that way we feel we encourage our children to develop positive self images, build self reliant attitudes, and have happy, valued, and loved dispositions.

We believe that children should have the right to choose their own religion. We are also vegetarians. We let our chosen guardians know that it was important that the children be raised vegetarians until they were teenagers. At that time they could make their own decision to continue. As to religion, we thought it would be appropriate for them to choose what religious doctrine they wished to subscribe to when they become mature adults.

In addition, we gave our chosen guardians detailed instructions regarding how we want the children raised in the event of our death. This included subjects ranging from our values concerning education, to our philosophy on spiritual matters and family responsibilities.

Usually it is best to have your guardians separate from matters of insurance money. It is preferable to have separate trustees handle the money so that your guardians – who may be the world's greatest parents and worst money managers – have no perceived conflicts of interest. They should not be burdened with the additional responsibility of handling your money. The trustee simply makes a check payable to the guardians every month for the support, maintenance, health, and education of your children.

Sadly, I find that people usually spend more time figuring out what type of life insurance to purchase, or which lawyer to use to draw their estate plan, than the critical decision of who they'll choose as the guardians of their children.

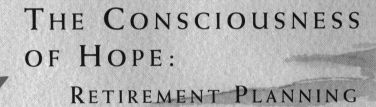

7

THE CONSCIOUSNESS
OF HOPE:
RETIREMENT PLANNING

"I hope my family will have a lifetime of financial security." "I hope to not lose it all to silly, ill-advised investing or poor health." "I am truly excited by my plans for retirement."

Planning for a secure retirement does take a certain amount of hope and faith, and the proper tools. These tools will manifest themselves through desire and the force which encourages us to create families and better the world we live in. Your future retirement security rests squarely on what you do prior to retirement. You must give your hope wings and take steps to assure your dreams come to fruition.

It's that simple – you must act on desire. "As you sow, so shall you reap."

Naturally, the devil in retirement planning is in the details. However, retiring with security requires a consistent savings schedule and the knowledge to use retirement planning and investment tools wisely.

The Taoist say a journey of a thousand miles begins with the first step; and the first step towards retirement requires establishing a "divine surplus" as described in The Gentle Budget. The next step is understanding a few basic tenets. Retirement means working:

if you want;
when you want;
where you want;
how you want;

and lastly, having the option to not work by allowing your built-up wealth to sustain you forever. Forever, for our purposes, is defined as however long you and your spouse and loved ones will need the money to provide you with an income stream.

In retirement, you must plan to live forever; this cannot be stressed enough. Many retirees of the late 1990s will live another 30 to 40 years or more, thanks to healthy lifestyles and modern medicine. Some of them will actually have retirement lives longer than their working lives.

Managing an investment portfolio to provide financial security for such a long period requires careful planning and an open-minded, goal-oriented approach designed to succeed no matter what the situation. This book will help you plan your investments so that you'll have the independence and peace of mind in the future that only a well managed portfolio can bring. While no person, book, or investment system can guarantee future success, you'll find that the idea of a "safety first" portfolio, and other principles herein, will provide a common sense approach, assuring you the security of winning by not losing.

In a world of perfect investments and perfect economies, there would be no inflation or investments with risk. Every investment would guarantee to provide retirees, widows, widowers, and endowments with a perpetual income stream to spend. The sober reality is that there are no perfect investments (despite what your broker or investment seller may tell you) and inflation is real. Risk exists in every one of your investments due to "the bad guys": inflation, fraud, poor markets, bankruptcy, stupidity, greed, taxes, complacency, or bad timing.

So how do you succeed as an investor with all these potential downfalls? One of the best ways is planning to win by studying the enemy and knowing their weaknesses and strengths. And again, by not losing.

Most investors bury their head in the sand. They refuse to look objectively at the inherent risks in all investments which would compel them to develop a risk minimization strategy. Unsuccessful investors scarcely acknowledge that investments do flounder for unexplained reasons. They use an oversimplified approach pushed by unscrupulous brokers, bankers, CFPs, CPAs, lawyers, and lucky friends.

Other investors wisely protect themselves from the aforementioned speculative investment sellers, but ignore inflation. Inflation can be a devastating blow to financial well-being by creeping up on a portfolio and slowly debilitating the investment's ability to provide a favorable income stream.

In 1973, the endowment trustees of Harvard University

were confronted with rising costs, inflation, stagnant or diminishing government support, and uncertain financial markets. They were intent on managing money to assure perpetual, long-term security while stressing conservative spending policies, so they adopted a policy based upon the assumption that:

1. Inflation would average 4%.
2. The University's costs would increase 6% per year.
3. The endowment's total return would be around 8% with a portfolio 65% in equities and 35% in bonds.
4. Gifts and bequests would average 2%.

The trustees decided to spend 4% of the endowment's market value, annually. They based their annual spending target on a prevailing market value of assets, so that spending would fluctuate based upon the "swinging" value of the portfolio. They also set up a stabilization fund to save excess earnings in good years (to be distributed in poor years).

My rule of thumb is to never draw on your portfolio over 6% (unless you are in dire need of the funds) while realizing that the long-term consequences of drawing from 4% to 6% and over may adversely affect your purchasing power over time. For portfolios that are actively managed under a strategy designed to avoid over-valued assets and favor their under-valued counterparts (the Do-It-Yourself market cycle portfolio with 35% risk tolerance in Chapter 3), 6% is okay; but for an extremely conservative portfolio, 4% may be too high.

When I was a child my mother would kiss me on the forehead as she left to visit my grandmother saying, "Your grandma's seventy-six and she'll probably not make it to seventy-seven, so this is likely to be the last time I'll get to see her."

And each year she would drive the twelve hour journey to a small coal mining town in southeastern Ohio. This went on for 20 years. Later, as I became involved as a student in the investment

"Divine Love always has met and always will meet every human need."

MARY BAKER EDDY

business, Mom would remark how awful my uncle was because he would only allow Grandma her stock dividends to live on and never let her spend the principal. She would tell me how Uncle Frank was worried about inflation and he firmly believed that Grandma's money had to be managed as if she would live forever. So he invested in stocks whose dividends tended to increase every few years, and remarkably, Grandma always had more money to spend each year to offset inflation. Well, Grandma lived to ninety-six, and those last few years my mom would say, "You know Paul, I used to argue with Uncle Frank about how he managed Mom's money as if she would live forever, and he was right."

When my grandmother died and mom inherited her share of stocks, I was amazed to see how well my uncle had chosen securities for her portfolio. There were many different companies in industries that grew over the years, and they all paid dividends. My uncle had carefully monitored Grandma's portfolio to

prosperity and security. His efforts and willingness to stand up against my mom and avoid dipping into her principal had been a great service to the family. Had they dipped into her principal at age seventy-six, not only would Grandma have run out of money by the end of her life, she also would have had much less to spend after a few years.

Preserve Your Earning Power

Conceptually you must look at your portfolio like a farmer views an egg-laying chicken. You wouldn't want to eat the chicken (principle) nor would you want to eat all of the eggs (income), so that some of them will, in turn, hatch, and eventually lay more eggs (help offset inflation).

In order not to utilize any principle and preserve some interest earned within your account, each month you should draw between .3% and .5% (depending on your volatility constraint, which translates on a yearly level to never more than 6% for even the most aggressive investor). **Figure 7.1** shows exactly what $100,000 will pay investors of varying levels of aggressiveness. Retired investors should favor equity income funds for the equity/stock/growth portion of their portfolio. Remember, risk tolerance is more a philosophical issue than a financial one.

Thus, if your Do-It-Yourself portfolio was managed under a 25% volatility constraint, your $100,000 portfolio should have an income constraint of $450 monthly; usually this amount is adjusted annually, so that if your $100,000 grew to $110,000 in its second year, your monthly income would grow to $495.

Based upon historical studies, this portfolio strategy could, over time, slowly be eroded by inflation, though it will depend on your portfolio's overall performance. A 1% differentiation in performance – year after year – will be noticed very little in the short term, but over 20 to 30 years, it will have a dramatic impact. This is where discipline pays off. A diligent review of your mutual fund holdings, with information provided by Lipper and Morningstar, will help ensure long-term growth.

Depending on your tax situation, we generally recommend that our retiring clients pay off all debt and pay cash for everything. This will keep you from investing borrowed money. If you have the assets, pay off your home, auto, second home, et cetera, before you retire.

Retirement Tools

There are many incredibly effective retirement tools to help you achieve retirement security. Millions of us are covered by 401(k)s, TSAs, and 403(b)s which

7.1 Maximum Percentage to Draw on Investment

Volatility Constraint	% to draw annually	Monthly	$100,000 would pay
35% Aggressive Investor	6%	.05%	$500 Monthly
25% Balanced Investor	5.4%	.045%	$450 Monthly
15% Yield Investor	4.8%	.04%	$400 Monthly
5% Capital Preservation	3.6%	.03%	$300 Monthly

allow us to take funds out our pay-checks and deposit them in a "Good Retirement Karma Box," all with tax benefits that truly were designed by a financial angel.

For self-employed savers, there are eight plans for you to consider, each with characteristics that should benefit you nicely.

Some lucky souls will qualify for IRA Plans which have many great benefits. All of the plans are described on the following pages in enough detail to guide you.

The Roth & Deductible IRAs

Beginning in 1998, you will be eligible to choose between two different IRA accounts: Deductible IRAs and the Roth

---

7.2 Why Use Qualified Retirement Plans

Contributions Are Currently Tax Deductible

EXAMPLE

$1000.00 Placed in Plan
-400.00 Tax saved at 40% tax bracket
$600.00 Net cost to build net worth by $1000.00

Earnings on Plan Assets Grow Tax Free

EXAMPLE

$1000.00 monthly @ 6% not taxed   = $462,000 in 20 years
                                          $1,004,000 in 30 years
$600.00 monthly @ 6% less 40% tax = 3.6% net return
                                          $350,000 in 20 years
                                          $646,640 in 30 years

---

Lots of Money in Retirement Plan = Lots of Income at Retirement

EXAMPLE

$1,000.00 monthly @ 6%   = $462,000 in 20 years   = $2,310/mo @ 6%
                                 $1,004,000 in 30 years = $5,020/mo@ 6%
$600.00 monthly @ 6%   = 3.6% net return
                                 $350,000 in 20 years   = $1,750/mo @ 6%
                                 $646,640 in 30 years   = $3,233/mo @ 6%

Note: This illustration is over-simplified; however, it accurately highlights the tax benefits of a retirement plan – not to mention the liability protection.

7.3 Samples of Monthly Investments and Various Rates of Return

$150 Monthly at Various Rates of Return

% RATE	YEARS	5	10	20	30	35
12.5%		$12,415	$35,537	$158,774	$586,050	$1,103,850
10%		$11,615	$30,727	$113,905	$339,073	$569,495
6%		$10,465	$24,581	$69,306	$150,677	$213,706
0%		$9,000	$18,000	$36,000	$54,000	$63,000

$500 Monthly at Various Rates of Return

% RATE	YEARS	5	10	20	30	35
12.5%		$41,386	$118,456	$529,246	$1,953,804	$ 3,679,792
10%		$38,718	$102,422	$379,684	$1,130,243	$1,898,319
6%		$34,885	$81,939	$231,020	$502,257	$712,355
0%		$30,000	$60,000	$120,000	$180,000	$210,000

$2,000 Monthly at Various Rates of Return

% RATE	YEARS	5	10	20	30	35
12.5%		$165,545	$473,826	$2,116,987	$7,815,218	$14,719,170
10%		$154,874	$409,689	$1,518,737	$4,520,975	$7,593,276
6%		$139,540	$327,758	$924,081	$2,009,030	$2,849,420
0%		$120,000	$240,000	$480,000	$720,000	$840,000

"Trust in Allah - but tie your camel first."

MUHAMMAD

7.4 Comparison of Plans for Retirement

	Plan Type	Contribution Limit	Investment Options	Suitability for Employees	Administrative Requirements	Key Advantage	Key Disadvantage	Who Should Consider
SELF-SPONSORED PLAN	IRA	Up to the lesser of $2000 or 100% of earned income if eligible	Stocks, Bonds, Annuities, Mutual Funds, Real Estate, CDs, (No Life Insurance)	Personal plan: not designed for employee benefit purposes	None	Completely your own plan	$2000 contribution limit	Anyone who qualifies
SELF EMPLOYED PLAN	Defined Benefit Plan (DBP)	Maximum benefit is 100% of pay up to $125,000	Same as profit sharing	Best for older employees due to guaranteed benefit	Same as profit sharing plus actuarial certification	Favors older participants	Complex administrative requirements for employer	All eligible employees are automatically enrolled
	Money Purchase Plan (MMP)	25% of pay or $30,000 whichever is less	Same as profit sharing	Best for younger employees if maximum contribution made	Same as profit sharing	Larger contribution limit than other defined contribution plans	No contribution flexibility	All eligible employees are automatically enrolled
	Profit Sharing	15% of overall pay up to $30,000 individually	Same as IRA, i.e..generally managed portfolios	Very good for work incentive, appeals to younger employers	Document, annual government filing, employee reports	Flexible contributions	Provides limited benefits for older participants	All eligible employees are automatically enrolled
	SEP (IRA)	15% of earned income or $30,000 whichever is less	Same as IRA	Limited by restricted plan options	Simple document no annual filing	Self employed plan with least paperwork	Must include part-time employees	Employer with maximum IRA and no employees
	SIMPLE (IRA)	Up to first $6000 of earned income	Same as IRA	Best for small business/under $60,000 income	Document, annual meeting, some tracking	Largest deduction for owners with limited income	Must match employee contribution up to 3%	Smaller employer with low income or with side income
EMPLOYEE/EMPLOYER VOLUNTEER PLAN	401k	$9500 in employee contributions up to 15% overall	Same as IRA, i.e., generally managed portfolios	Best for younger employees if maximum contribution made	Document, annual government filing, employee reports	Employee investment direction, positive employee perception	Complex administrative requirements for employer	All eligible employees should automatically be enrolled
	403b	25% or $30,000, $9500 can be from salary reduction	Mutual funds and annuities	Only option for most employees of non-profit hospitals or schools	Modest	Modest excellent tax favored wealth creator	$9500 limit from salary reduction	All eligible employees of non-profit organizations

IRA, both of which provide important tax savings.

Unless your earnings are modest, and you are covered by a qualified retirement plan, you will not qualify for the deductible IRA. On the other hand, if your spouse is not covered by a qualified retirement plan and your adjusted gross income is under $150,000, your spouse may be eligible to fund up to $2,000 in a tax deductible IRA.

The new Roth IRA does not give an upfront tax deduction; however, the IRA does offer something that many feel is even more valuable: tax-free withdrawals of both contributions and investment earnings if the money is withdrawn after the account has been established for five years and after the account owner reaches $59^1/_2$. The Roth IRA may permit tax- and penalty-free withdrawals before that age, owing to the death or disability of the owner, or the first time purchase of a home.

You can still be covered by a qualified retirement plan at work to qualify for a Roth IRA; eligibility is dependent upon income

limits, however. You can make a full $2,000 contribution to a Roth IRA in 1998 if you are a single taxpayer with an adjusted gross income that is less than $95,000. Couples, filing joint returns, may own non-deductible Roth IRAs if their adjusted gross income is $150,000 or less. There are reduced contributions allowed for single taxpayers with an adjusted gross income of between $95,000 and $110,000, and for couples with an adjusted gross income of between $150,000 and $160,000. Anyone eligible should take maximum advantage of Roth IRAs.

For the non-deductible Roth IRAs, tax free withdrawals are not allowed within the first five taxable years, beginning with the first taxable year when a contribution was made. Funds may be distributed from a Roth IRA (tax free) on or after reaching $59^1/_2$. Distributions can be directed to a beneficiary of the individual's estate, after the death of the individual, if the individual is disabled, or for a qualified special purpose, such as buying a first home.

The maximum annual contri-

bution to a Roth IRA is $2,000. This amount can be reduced further if a contribution is made to another IRA maintained for the individual's benefit. Contributions to the Roth IRA can also be made after the individual reaches age $70^1/_2$ (unlike the deductible IRA). Taxpayers may rollover amounts from an existing IRA to a Roth IRA. Any taxable amount rolled over from a current IRA, however, must be included as taxable income over the next four tax years, if done in 1998, and all at once for tax years after 1998. This option is available for taxpayers whose adjusted gross income is under $100,000.

If your employer is compassionate enough to offer a 403b, TSA, 401k or SIMPLE IRA, by all means take advantage. Try to dedicate at least 10% of your income toward your retirement plan to help quickly build your nest egg. Review Chapter 4 for investment guidance, and of course, plan to live forever...

LEARNING TO ASK:
FINANCIAL EXPERTS & PROFESSIONALS

8

"What's your spiritual attitude toward money?"

This was how a potential new client chose to engage me in a conversation about investing, before he made a decision about who he would hire. He had inherited quite a bit of money and felt very strongly, on a philosophical level, that he wanted a financial advisor who would do more than just make him money.

I sat back and contemplated how to answer. I knew that he had already decided to use me, but his question was the most intriguing I'd heard from a client in twenty years.

"You know I won't buy tobacco, alcohol, pornography, and other companies that do crummy stuff. We also send out a letter to all the companies we invest in asking them to adopt the Caux Principles of ethical business practices."

He nodded and said "I know all that, but what I want to know is. . ."

Finally, an hour or so later we came to an understanding and I am a better person for it.

This client loves his job, loves his family, and finds the whole world interesting and beautiful. Like most of us, he gets frustrated by ignorance and insensitivity, but is able to stay balanced through it all. Upon receiving the inheritance he bought a book and thought about doing his own money management. Then he talked to an insurance agent and a stock broker, but realized he didn't want to hire someone who earned commissions just to offer him advice. He had been referred to me by a few of his friends but was concerned about the "fee" part of our "fee only" philosophy.

Finding a financial advisor who can oversee your investments is often harder than finding a priest, minister, guru, rabbi, or Imago therapist. And in much the same way one can get along spiritually without the influence of a religious leader, it is also very possible to manage your finances alone. In fact, if your only option is to get your advice from a commissioned person, even if they agree to advise you for a fee and no commissions, opt against them and do it yourself. Why fee-only all the time? It's simple. An advisor can't serve two masters: you and commissions. If an advisor recognizes even a hint of conflict between the investments they choose and commissions earned, they should go fee-only all the time or they are violating their principles for money.

Even if planning to Do-It-Yourself, it is important that you find competent professionals to assist you with the implementation of your financial goals. This will be much easier if you have previously worked with a financial planner. Ultimately, you will need outside experts in various fields to assist you in drawing your financial plan into action. For example, for a will or a trust to be drawn, the skills of a good estate planning or tax attorney are necessary.

Choosing a professional can be difficult, but their influence is an integral part of your financial security. A poorly qualified or domineering professional can raise havoc with even the best drawn financial plan.

Many years ago, I remember asking an accountant why he hadn't recommended that his client incorporate in order to set up a more favorable retirement plan. He responded, "I know it would save a lot of money in taxes, but he (the client) would just spend it on frivolous things. He would waste money, so what's the use of incorporating him, or using tax-saving strategies?"

The client came to me (after thirty years with the same accountant) because he owed many years in back taxes. By simply rearranging his financial situation, we were able to get his debt situation under control, instigate a savings plan for retirement, and thereby greatly reduce his stress level.

An insurance agent, who called himself a financial advisor, recommended his client buy a large whole life policy to take care of his need for disability income, life insurance, retirement funds, and to build liquid cash. The agent had his client pay for this insurance benefit on a non-deductible basis. When I asked why he hadn't recommended that the client purchase term insurance, a real disability policy, and put the rest of the money into a tax-favored retirement plan, his reply was, "No one can make any money just selling term insurance and earning the small commissions on securities that would go into a retirement plan."

Each of these advisors – if they could be called advisors – had known their clients for quite a number of years. Needless to say, these relationships were costly to the individual's financial health. Your success or failure is dependent upon your understanding of how the pieces of a financial plan fit together, and whether or not you receive sound financial advice.

When you choose advisors, remember that you are the quarterback of your financial plan, and the game-plan should be in harmony with your philosophy and value system. Try to find like-minded team members (advisors) that are committed to excellence in their field. And, just like a quarterback, you must also know

the duties and responsibilities of each of your advisors. You must always make the final decision – even if you hire a financial planner as your coach.

After many years of observation, I have concluded that most people choose professionals without understanding the issues and responsibilities at stake. Hire a professional that will commit to giving you accurate, unbiased advice. When you fully consider the dire consequences (destitution, tax fraud, liability, et cetera), there should be no mistaking the seriousness of your hiring decisions.

To find suitable professionals, I suggest that you seek the advice of friends or acquaintances (that appear to be financially successful, pragmatic, and intelligent) to see who they use. Ask a number of people so that you get a varying list of professionals to interview.

With a notepad in hand and the following list of questions, (page 90) call the prospect and ask them to lunch, or interview them by phone.

In addition, you should also ask your prospective investment

Professional Checklist of Questions:

1. Describe your average client.
2. How long have you been in business? How long in this specialized or specific area?
3. How many clients do you have?
4. Do you have any one client who represents more than 10% of your income in the last 12 months?
5. Do you plan on staying in this profession? How long?
6. Do you consider yourself an advisor or number cruncher?
7. What business/professional associations do you belong to?
8. Can you give me two professional character references?
9. Can you give me two clients to call as references who have been clients for the last 10 years?
10. How do you get most of your business?
11. Who is your "ideal" client?
12. What determines your pricing?
13. Is your fee negotiable?
14. How much will you handle on my account *(versus your associate)*?
15. Have you ever been bankrupt?
16. Do you have business goals? What are they?
17. How do you run your business?
18. Do I have access to all documents in your file about my specific situation?
19. What assurances do I have of complete confidentiality?
20. How long has your staff been with you and who are they?
21. Do you like your job?
22. Are you one of those guys who reads professional journals at home for pleasure?
23. Have you ever been treated for substance abuse, or been in jail?
24. What is your spiritual attitude towards money?
25. Has your firm adopted the CAUX Principals?
26. What are your thoughts on socially responsible investing?
27. Have you read *Zenvesting*?

advisor the following five questions:

1. What is your firm's investment philosophy?
2. You are a "fee-only" advisor. Why?
3. What makes you better than the people down the street?
4. If your advisor serves a national or international clientele: Can you still be effective as my advisor with other clients scattered all over the world?
5. Who backs you up if you go on vacation, die, or become disabled?

Your initial goal should be to let him or her do all the talking, while you ask questions. And do not be afraid to ask difficult questions, because they will get you the answers and the responses that will help you judge the character of the individual. For example, if you know the advisor has gone through a divorce, ask them whether they have possible relocation plans. Or if a new receptionist is answering the phone,

find out what happened with the old one. When you ask these questions, also pay attention to body language; if they hedge or get uncomfortable, ask follow-up questions that are specific to the sensitive issues. Be merciless, because you deserve the best. A good professional will respect you for your candidness and desire to hire a quality advisor.

You will need expert advice in six specific fields for your financial plan. Not necessarily six different people, but advice on the following issues:

1. Law.
2. Accounting.
3. Financial planning.
4. Investing.
5. Retirement planning.
6. Insurance.

These advisors can often be found within the same office as your financial planner.

Financial Planner

A financial planner is one of the most important professionals you'll choose. They should address your entire financial situ-

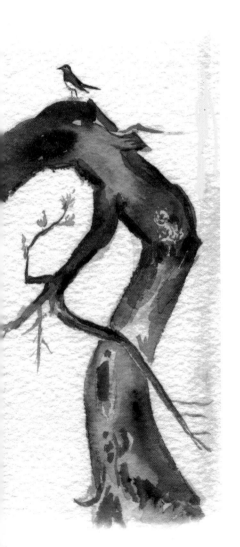

ation and complement your other advisors. It doesn't matter what size firm they work for; choose a financial planner based firstly on individual credentials and secondly on the back-up services of the company.

Attempt to find a financial planner whose philosophy and attitudes mesh with your own. Some firms have their business philosophy stated in writing for prospective clients in their company materials (ours is printed in **Figure 8.1**).

A financial planner may be compensated in any of three ways: fee for services (fee-only at all times), commission only for services, or a combination of fees and commissions.

The debate for top honors is a heated one. The fee-only financial planner will say that they will be much more objective because they work solely for a set fee, while the commission planner might argue that "the client is going to have to pay commissions anyway, so why not pay me the commission." Lastly, the fee and commission planner will stress that they can

lower fees because they are also earning commissions.

Financial planning should be oriented toward the long-term, where changes in tax laws, retirement planning laws, and the economy all come into play. Since investment cycles, insurance policies, and risk management techniques change over time, the financial planner should be compensated based on a relationship that is ongoing for many years, without the conflict created by commissions.

The relationship that you have with a financial planner will develop over time, and the trust should come only when your financial planner has delivered. You should not be forced into a relationship because you paid a large fee or commission upfront and feel compelled to get your money's worth. It is important to maintain an equitable relationship – one committed to the long-term. If you currently have an attorney, accountant, insurance agent, or an investment advisor that has given you sound advice over the years, and are about to

8.1 Investment Philosophy

FINANCIAL & INVESTMENT MANAGEMENT GROUP, LTD.

OUR INVESTMENT PHILOSOPHY IS
BASED UPON THE FOLLOWING BELIEF SYSTEM

We believe in the following:

1. That a perfect investment does not exist for all investment cycles and that to reduce risk, assets should be re-allocated to avoid overvalued assets and favor undervalued assets accordingly during each financial cycle. Thus, we believe in active portfolio management.

2. That it is important for a money manager to discipline himself to remain flexible and creative. At Financial & Investment Management Group, Ltd. (FIMG), we use both fundamental and technical analysis in making our investment and asset allocation decisions.

3. That diversification should be used carefully to reduce risks and increase rewards by allocating investment portfolios as follows:
   a) Among asset classes; i.e., stocks, bonds, money market funds, etc.
   b) Within each asset class; through owning many different investments within each asset class or through the use of diversified companies, mutual funds, annuities, or other investments with built-in diversification.
   c) Through management style; by utilizing outside advisors to assist in making investment and asset allocation decisions.
   d) Globally; through exploring investment opportunities worldwide.

4. That patience and perseverance are essential qualities of a money manager. A successful investor must keep a long-term horizon and avoid getting caught up in the mania of the markets. This mania is caused by rapid changes in investor psychology due to real or perceived economic, societal, or financial events.

8.1 Investment Philosophy continued

5. That during certain periods in the market it is wiser to emphasize capital preservation, while during other periods greater emphasis must be placed on capital growth. At all times, a manager should carefully search the world for risk adjusted bargain investments for client portfolios.

6. That it is important for a money manager to minimize all costs associated with investing. FIMG achieves this by trading at substantially discounted commissions, using no-load funds with low expense ratios, and allocating trades to brokers specializing in certain investment areas.

7. That to be totally objective, a money manager must be compensated only on a fee-basis. No commissions or any other transaction-related remuneration should be received by the manager. FIMG is strictly a fee-only manager.

8. That a money manager should have the training, temperament, experience, and resources available which will promote success in their field. A manager "must manage," enjoy the process of management, and have passion, commitment, and love for the investment business.

9. That money managers making specific investment decisions regarding client portfolios should be accessible to their clients to discuss strategy, market outlook, conditions, and so on.

10. That our primary goal is to maintain the highest degree of integrity, ethics, and quality in working with our clients, employees, business partners, and service providers.

11. In client confidentiality and have a firm "no exceptions" policy stating that no information will be sold or shared with anyone, except as required by law, or with the clients' express permission.

This is the philosophy of Financial & Investment Management Group, Ltd. We believe that if you find this makes sound investment sense, then you will consider us as your investment manager.

interview a general financial planner, invite that trusted advisor to sit in on the meeting. Let them assist you with the questioning process so that you are sure of what that person can do.

Stock brokers, investment advisors, and insurance agents are not money managers (or financial planners). They are salespeople who get paid to sell you things. The inherent conflicts in this relationship undermine the very nature of an industry predicated on sound, objective advice. Don't trust your assets or financial well-being to anyone who can get a commission for selling you investment ideas or products. Hire a Security and Exchange Commission, registered, strictly fee-only, independent money manager.

Read your prospective advisor's philosophy statement and SEC/ADV disclosure forms, then have your investment manager show you an existing account that will be similar to how he or she feels your portfolio should be structured. Get references from at least three people who have been

clients for at least six years.

Always keep your assets with you as beneficial owner. Only allow your advisor the right to make buy and sell decisions on your portfolio, and to vote your proxies on management issues in the companies you've invested in. Make sure that you know what your manager is buying or selling. Look over the information and then, to avoid clutter, throw it away or recycle it. Keep only your monthly and quarterly statements.

Don't use expensive wrap-fee programs (where all commissions, management, and custodial fees are charged at once). While they are very popular on Wall Street as a way to control the costs of investing, they usually work out to be very expensive. Use brokers that will let you trade at a maximum of $.10 per share. We pay about $.05 and never buy front-end commission load or back-end load mutual funds. In the past there was some justification for buying load funds; today it is unnecessary.

Your fee-only investment advisor should do everything

Some say that my teaching
is nonsense.
Others call it lofty but impractical.
But to those who have looked inside
themselves, this nonsense makes
perfect sense.
And to those who put it into practice,
this loftiness has roots that go deep.

I have just three things to teach:
   simplicity, patience,
   compassion.
   These three
   are your greatest treasures.

Simple in actions and in thoughts,
you return to the source of being.
Patient with both friends and enemies,
you accord with the way things are.
Compassionate toward yourself,
you reconcile all beings in the world.

TAO TE CHING

possible to control costs. If your advisor does not seem deeply committed to this, then it is time to address a possible change.

Also, make a commitment to find a money manager who feels as strongly as you do about developing a socially responsible portfolio. If they do not spend a majority of time researching enlightened companies, then they are wasting your time and money analyzing other investments.

The top attributes I look for in prospective managers are passion, experience, and a love for the investment business. I firmly believe that anyone who truly subscribes to these three qualities will naturally embrace a fee-only philosophy. This should include being a member of certain associations that have the strictest competence and ethical requirements, and a willingness to discuss your portfolio any time you wish.

General Attorney

A general attorney should help you with your real estate transactions, and other legal matters. They should advise you on simple will and trust arrangements, and any contracts that you may enter into. If your attorney has training in tax areas, they can help you to analyze complex estate planning issues, the tax structure of real estate, or other tax-sheltered deals to assure they will comply with current tax law. If your general attorney does not offer specialized tax services, ask for a recommendation. Don't force your tax attorney to do general legal work, nor is it a good idea to make your general practice attorney do the majority of your legal work. For example, if you need to hire an attorney to protect you in a lawsuit, you would want the best trial attorney that you could find. Even though you may trust and respect your regular attorney, ask for a referral to a trial attorney.

Accountants

For general purposes, it is important that we distinguish between the two types of accountants. The first type is one that takes information and puts it down on paper (so that you can file, for example, a tax return), or serves as your bookkeeper. These accountants are not advisors, even if they promote themselves as a CPA or "advisor". Indeed, you should never force them into the role of being your advisor, since their main job is to crunch numbers (a worthy pursuit in itself).

An accountant that serves as your advisor is the second type. They should help you monitor your income to keep you out of a negative tax situation and review any tax strategy that may be recommended by your financial planner, investment advisor, realtor, or retirement planning advisor. Both the retirement planning and investment areas are specialized fields that require the qualified expertise of a proven professional.

A good tax advisor will save you thousands of dollars in taxes. Finding one that is pragmatic and willing to spend some time learning about your situation is one of the shrewdest financial planning maneuvers you can make. CPAs also make great financial planners, especially if they have an MBA, and/or CFP, and the experience in the financial planning business.

Insurance Advisors

The ideal person to serve as your life, health, and disability advisor is your financial planner. It is very important for you to find one who believes that insurance should be simple and efficient – just enough to cover you adequately. Take an especially close look at why they recommend one policy over another. And, like any other professional on your team, your insurance advisor should be open and accepting of criticism, and fee-only all the time.

Casualty Insurance Advisor

The chapter on insurance details most of the types of insurance you will need. A key ally to assist in obtaining coverage is your local insurance agent. They should manage and structure your home, auto, liability, catastrophe, and umbrella policies. It is convenient to have a local casualty insurance advisor for the errant baseball through your front window or when lightning strikes.

Keep your agent up-to-date regarding changes in your household. For example, when you put up a new satellite dish, a rider should be added to your homeowners policy, et cetera.

The MBA

At least one of your advisors should have a Masters in Business Administration (MBA). MBAs have a special understanding of business and portfolio management due to their ability to evaluate the common characteristics and management at various companies, to size up their predisposition for success. The Certified Financial Planner (CFP), or CPA with an MBA may be best suited to stand tall as a top advisor.

Other Advisors

The other types of advisors that may be needed occasionally are bank trust officers, plan administrators, and realtors. Keep in mind that these advisors are specialists and are not used in all situations, and you must go to them with specific goals. Use the questionaire on page 90 to guide you to all of your advisors and your long term relationships should be positive.

A LAST WORD

Financial success is the result of right effort and creatively engaging skills used in the production of something necessary.

If we are to grow in our awareness of the global economic reality, it is necessary for all compassionate Zen students to expand their financial understanding beyond a personal level.

Look at healthy communities. They are either democratic or ruled by an enlightened leadership who encourages creativity. People are productive and happy to be involved in work and relationships that benefit the community. Economics is the fundamental reality of their relationships.

Envy, greed and laziness are the three arch enemies of both community and individual. They are democracy restricters, hampering individuals from pursuing beneficial relationships.

The wise leader says to the lazy: please work; to the greedy: please share; and to the envious: go away if you are unwilling to cooperate.

Benevolent leaderships work in communities and businesses because people are free to vote with their feet – by leaving if they choose. Even with its perceived shortcomings, democratic capitalism is the ideal Zen economic system because it allows people the most freedoms and choices.

Democracies are typically made up of entities such as states, counties, towns, businesses where there is open communication between leaders and stakeholders.

Greed is manifested in capitalism through a misallocation of resources. But greed causes havoc in capitalism, Marxism, socialism, and dictatorships, alike. Chronically unemployed (uninspired) workers live off the efforts of others by utilizing the arguments that "there are no good jobs," or "I'm too old to get an education," but the issue is laziness, regardless of the economic system.

A Zen Master in his late nineties fell ill and bedridden. He refused to eat, citing the explanation, "In our community, to eat today, you must work today."

His students pleaded with him, "Master, we will share. Please eat." To which the Master replied, "To eat today, work today."

The students were unable to persuade him until they finally lifted the Master's bed and placed it in the garden; tossing out the scarecrow.

Productive again, the Master spent his last days throwing rocks at crows and munching on juicy tomatoes fresh off the vine.

If we are not producing, serving and helping because of our own complacency, there is serious danger of becoming sad and depressed. A community caught up in a pattern of such despondency will quickly deteriorate. That is why the wise Zen Master was so resistant to take from his community without right effort. He did not wish to chance the possibility of group depression.

The bountiful river of life demands work and balance. Our personal success in living in the real economic world is no matter of luck and happenstance. Right effort, creatively engaging skills and the production of something useful leads to happiness, financial success and a healthy community.

All students of Dharma should understand economics as a natural course of their studies. When reduced down to a few key tenets, personal economics becomes comically simple; serve others, create services and products that help others, work every day, avoid envy, breath, and smile.

As I breathe and smile through out my day, I will serve others. I will be aware of the needs of others, including all people, all animals, our living earth and all sentient beings. I am conscious that all individuals are working out their own karma. Envy, jealousy, and intolerance must not cloud my desire to love and serve. I realize that peace must begin with me, so I will treat my body, mind and spirit with respect. I will allow myself and others to change. I know that today I have the power of choice and can decide to embrace that which brings harmony, love, prosperity, and joy to my world.

INVESTOR RESOURCES

On the following pages you will find Investor Worksheets and a list of social investing associations, newsletters and websites. We provide these sections for guidance and with the hope that they will aid you in determining both the type of investor you choose to be and the kinds of investments you wish to make.

Aggressive Portfolio

3% Yields 35% volatility
6 YEAR TIME FRAME

Portfolio Registration

_____

Custodial Broker _____

Phone Number _____

Account # _____

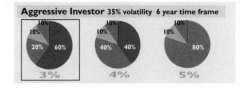

Aggressive Investor 35% volatility 6 year time frame

60% Balanced Funds	Approx %	Amt.Invested	Date
1.	%		
2.	%		
3.	%		
4.	%		
5.	%		
6.	%		

20% Stock Funds			
1.	%		
2.	%		
3.	%		
4.	%		

NO BOND FUNDS NO MONEY MARKET FUNDS

10% Gold & Natural Resource Funds			
1.	%		
2.	%		

10% International Stock Funds			
1.	%		
2.	%		

Notes

Growth Portfolio

3% Yields 30% volatility
5 YEAR TIME FRAME

Portfolio Registration

_____

Custodial Broker _____

Phone Number _____

Account # _____

50% Balanced Funds	Approx %	Amt.Invested	Date
1.	%		
2.	%		
3.	%		
	%		
10% Stock Funds	%		
1.	%		
2.			
10% Bond Funds	%		
1.	%		
2.	%		
	%		
10% Money Market Funds			
1.			
10% Gold & Natural Resource Funds			
1.	%		
2.	%		
10% International Stock Funds			
1.	%		
2.	%		

Notes

Balanced Portfolio

3% Yields 25% volatility
5 YEAR TIME FRAME

Portfolio Registration

_____

Custodial Broker _____

Phone Number _____

Account # _____

Balanced Investor 25% volatility 5 year time frame

3%   4%   5%

10% Balanced Funds	Approx %	Amt. Invested	Date
1.	%		
2.	%		
10% Stock Funds	%		
1.	%		
2.	%		
20% Bond Funds			
1.	%		
2.	%		
3.	%		
40% Money Market Funds			
1.	%		
10% Gold & Natural Resource Funds			
1.	%		
2.	%		
10% International Stock Funds			
1.	%		
2.	%		

Notes

Yield Portfolio

3% Yields 15% volatility
4 YEAR TIME FRAME

Portfolio Registration

_____

Custodial Broker   _____

Phone Number   _____

Account #   _____

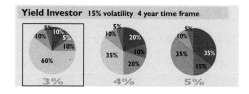

Yield Investor 15% volatility 4 year time frame

10% Balanced Funds	Approx %	Amt.Invested	Date
1.	%		
2.	%		

5% Stock Funds			
1.	%		
2.	%		

10% Bond Funds			
1.	%		
2.	%		
3.	%		

60% Money Market Funds			
1.	%		

10% Gold & Natural Resource Funds			
1.	%		
2.	%		

5% International Stock Funds			
1.	%		
2.	%		

Notes

WORKSHEET

Capital Preservation Portfolio

3% Yields 5% volatility
1 YEAR TIME FRAME

Portfolio Registration

_____

Custodial Broker _____

Phone Number _____

Account # _____

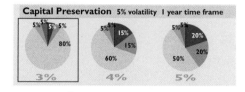

Capital Preservation 5% volatility 1 year time frame

5% Balanced Funds		Approx %	Amt.Invested	Date
1.		%		
2.		%		
3.		%		

NO STOCK FUNDS

5% Bond Funds

1.		%		
2.		%		
3.		%		

80% Money Market Funds

1.		%		

5% Gold & Natural Resource Funds

1.		%		
2.		%		
3.		%		

5% International Stock Funds

1.		%		
2.		%		

Notes

Aggressive Portfolio

4% Yields 35% volatility
6 YEAR TIME FRAME

Portfolio Registration

_____

Custodial Broker _____

Phone Number _____

Account # _____

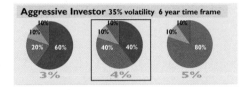

40% Balanced Funds	Approx %	Amt.Invested	Date
1.	%		
2.	%		
3.	%		
4.	%		

40% Stock Funds			
1.	%		
2.	%		
3	%		
4.	%		

NO BOND FUNDS NO MONEY MARKET FUNDS

10% Gold & Natural Resource Funds			
1.	%		
2.	%		
3.	%		

10% International Stock Funds			
1.	%		
2.	%		
3.	%		

Notes

WORKSHEET

Growth Portfolio

4% Yields 30% volatility
5 YEAR TIME FRAME

Portfolio Registration

_____

Custodial Broker _____

Phone Number _____

Account # _____

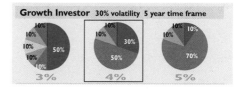

Growth Investor 30% volatility 5 year time frame

3%   4%   5%

30% Balanced Funds	Approx %	Amt. Invested	Date
1.	%		
2.	%		
3.	%		
4.			

50% Stock Funds	Approx %	Amt. Invested	Date
	%		
1.	%		
2.	%		
3.	%		
4.	%		
5.	%		
6.	%		

NO BOND FUNDS NO MONEY MARKET FUNDS

10% Gold & Natural Resource Funds	Approx %	Amt. Invested	Date
1.	%		
2.	%		

10% International Stock Funds	Approx %	Amt. Invested	Date
1.	%		
2.	%		

Notes

Balanced Portfolio

4% Yields 25% volatility
5 YEAR TIME FRAME

Portfolio Registration

_____

Custodial Broker   _____

Phone Number   _____

Account #   _____

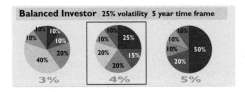

Balanced Investor 25% volatility 5 year time frame

25% Balanced Funds	Approx %	Amt. Invested	Date
1.	%		
2.	%		
3.	%		
4.			
15% Stock Funds	%		
1.	%		
2.	%		
	%		
20% Bond Funds	%		
1.	%		
2.	%		
20% Money Market Funds			
1.			
2.			
	%		
10% Gold & Natural Resource Funds	%		
1.			
10% International Stock Funds	%		
1.	%		

Notes

Yield Portfolio

4% Yields 15% volatility
4 YEAR TIME FRAME

Portfolio Registration

_____

Custodial Broker _____

Phone Number _____

Account # _____

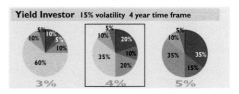

Yield Investor 15% volatility 4 year time frame

20% Balanced Funds	Approx %	Amt. Invested	Date
1.	%		
2.	%		
3.	%		

10% Stock Funds			
1.	%		
2.	%		

20% Bond Funds			
1.	%		
2.	%		
3.	%		

35% Money Market Funds			
1.	%		

10% Gold & Natural Resource Funds			
1.	%		
2.	%		

5% International Stock Funds			
1.	%		

Notes

Capital Preservation Portfolio

4% Yields 5% volatility
1 YEAR TIME FRAME

Portfolio Registration

_____

Custodial Broker _____

Phone Number _____

Account # _____

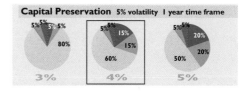

15% Balanced Funds	Approx %	Amt. Invested	Date
1.	%		
2.	%		
3.	%		
4.			
NO STOCK FUNDS	%		
	%		
15% Bond Funds			
1.			
2.	%		
3.	%		
	%		
60% Money Market Funds			
1.			
	%		
5% Gold & Natural Resource Funds			
1.			
2.	%		
	%		
5% International Stock Funds			
1.			
2.	%		

Notes

Aggressive Portfolio

5% Yields 35% volatility
6 YEAR TIME FRAME

Portfolio Registration

_____

Custodial Broker _____

Phone Number _____

Account # _____

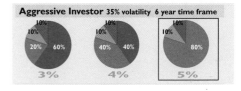

	Approx %	Amt. Invested	Date
NO BALANCED FUNDS			
80% Stock Funds			
1.	%		
2.	%		
3.	%		
4.	%		
5.	%		
6.	%		
7.	%		
NO BOND FUNDS NO MONEY MARKET FUNDS			
10% Gold & Natural Resource Funds			
1.	%		
2.	%		
3.	%		
10% International Stock Funds			
1.	%		
2.	%		
3.	%		

Notes

Growth Portfolio

5% Yields 30% volatility
5 YEAR TIME FRAME

Portfolio Registration

_____

Custodial Broker   _____

Phone Number   _____

Account #   _____

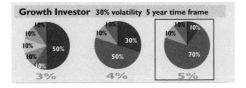

10% Balanced Funds	Approx %	Amt.Invested	Date
1.	%		
2.	%		
3.	%		

70% Stock Funds			
1.	%		
2.	%		
3.	%		
4.	%		
5.	%		
6.	%		
7.	%		

NO BOND FUNDS   NO MONEY MARKET FUNDS

10% Gold & Natural Resource Funds			
1.	%		
2.	%		

10% International Stock Funds			
1.	%		
2.	%		

Notes

Balanced Portfolio

5% Yields 25% volatility
5 YEAR TIME FRAME

Portfolio Registration

Custodial Broker

Phone Number

Account #

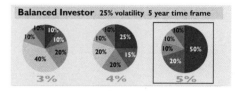

Balanced Investor 25% volatility 5 year time frame

3% 4% 5%

50% Balanced Funds	Approx %	Amt.Invested	Date
1.	%		
2.	%		
3.	%		
4.	%		

20% Stock Funds

1.	%		
2.	%		

10% Bond Funds

1.	%		
2.	%		

NO MONEY MARKET FUNDS

10% Gold & Natural Resource Funds

1.	%		
2.	%		

10% International Stock Funds

1.	%		
2.	%		

Notes

Yield Portfolio

5% Yields 15% volatility
4 YEAR TIME FRAME

Portfolio Registration

_____

Custodial Broker   _____

Phone Number _____

Account #   _____

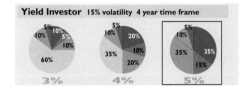

Yield Investor 15% volatility 4 year time frame

35% Balanced Funds	Approx %	Amt.Invested	Date
1.	%		
2.	%		
3.	%		
	%		
15% Stock Funds			
1.			
2.	%		
	%		
35% Bond Funds			
1.			
2.	%		
3.	%		

NO MONEY MARKET FUNDS

10% Gold & Natural Resource Funds			
1.	%		
2.	%		

5% International Stock Funds			
1.	%		
2.	%		

Notes

Capital Preservation Portfolio

5% Yields 5% volatility
1 YEAR TIME FRAME

Portfolio Registration

_____

Custodial Broker   _____

Phone Number   _____

Account #   _____

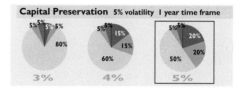

Capital Preservation 5% volatility 1 year time frame

3%   4%   5%

20% Balanced Funds	Approx %	Amt.Invested	Date
1.	%		
2.	%		
3.	%		
4.	%		

NO STOCK FUNDS

20% Bond Funds			
1.	%		
2.	%		
3.	%		

50% Money Market Funds			
1.	%		

5% Gold & Natural Resource Funds			
1.	%		
2.	%		

5% International Stock Funds			
1.	%		
2.	%		

Notes

SOCIAL INVESTING ASSOCIATIONS, NEWSLETTERS, AND WEB SITES

Co-Op America
1612 K Street N.W., Suite 600,
Washington, D.C. 20006
202.872.5307
Publishes a newsletter and two handbooks to help individuals and businesses address social and environmental issues.

Council on Economic Priorities
30 Irving Place, 9th Floor, New York, NY 10003
212.420.1133
Publishes CEP Research Report which rates all S&P 500 companies in various social categories.

Investor Responsibility Research Center
1350 Connecticut Avenue, N.W.,
Suite 70, Washington, D.C. 20036-1701
202.833.0700
Monitors corporate annual meetings through shareholder resolutions and publishes *Corporate Social Issues Reporter.*

The Impact Project
21 Linwood Street, Arlington, MA 02474
617.643.5678
Devoted to assisting the financially endowed with responsible charitable giving and investing. *More Than Money* newsletter.

Social Investment Forum
303.575.1597
Non-profit organization encouraging socially responsible investing among institutions.

Franklin Research & Development
711 Atlantic Avenue, 4th Floor,
Boston, MA 02111
617.423.6655
Publishes *Investing For A Better World* newsletter and rates companies on social issues.

Kinder, Lydenberg, Domini & Co., Inc.
129 Mt. Auburn Street, Cambridge, MA 02138
617.547.7479
Publishes *Domini Social Index* as a benchmark for evaluating companies on different social screens.

Clean Yield
P.O. Box 117, Greensboro, VT 05841
802.533.7178
Publishes newsletter focusing on stocks passing social responsibility screens.

The GreenMoney Journal
608 West Glass Avenue, Spokane, WA 99205
800.318.5725
Publishes quarterly journal on responsible business and investing.

Interfaith Center On Corporate Responsibility
475 Riverside Drive, Room 650, New York, NY 10115
212.870.2936
Publishes quarterly reports encouraging corporate social responsibility through shareholder activism.

Investors' Circle
3220 Sacramento Street, San Francisco, CA 94115
415.458-8703
Maintains a forum for accredited investors who are committing venture capital to socially responsible companies.

National Association of Community Development Loan Funds
924 Cherry Street, 2nd Floor, Philadelphia, PA 19107
215.923.4754
Publishes a directory of loan funds that lend money to low income community groups.

Social Venture Network
P.O. Box 29221,
San Francisco, CA 94109
415.561.6501 / www.svn.org
Oversees a growing contingent of 400 socially responsible business leaders, investors, and other visionaries. Conducts two annual conferences and publishes a newsletter.

Dollars And Sense
One Summer Street,
Somerville, MA 02143
617.628.8411.
Bi-monthly magazine on progressive economic issues and events.

Web Sites

www.coopamerica.org – Educational information and list of socially responsible mutual funds.

www.accesspt.com/cep.com – Database of companies rated against social screens.

www.greenmoney.com– Social and environmental information for consumers and investors

www.goodmoney.com – List of socially responsible funds and other information.

www.socialinvest.org – Mutual Fund Performance Chart and news on responsible investing.

www.simpleliving.org – "Equips people of faith to challenge consumerism, live justly and celebrate responsibly."

www.infact.org – A national grassroots organization dedicated to stopping the life-threatening abuses of transnational corporations.

Index